The Daily Telegraph

Quick Crossword Book
45

Also available in Pan Books

and in Macmillan

and for more titles visit www.panmacmillan.com

The Daily Telegraph
Quick Crossword Book
45

Pan Books
in association with *The Daily Telegraph*

First published in 2007 by Pan Books
This edition first published 2018 by Pan Books
an imprint of Pan Macmillan, a division of Macmillan Publishers Limited
Pan Macmillan, 20 New Wharf Road, London N1 9RR
Basingstoke and Oxford
Associated companies throughout the world
www.panmacmillan.com

In association with *The Daily Telegraph*

ISBN 978-1-5098-9376-8

Copyright © Telegraph Media Group Limited 2007

A CIP catalogue record for this book is available from the
British Library.

Visit **www.panmacmillan.com** to read more about all our books and to buy
them. You will also find features, author interviews and news of any author
events, and you can sign up for e-newsletters so that you're always first to hear
about our new releases.

ACROSS

1 Coil (4)
4 Big cat (7)
8 Choice food (8)
9 Tease; pectoral bone (3)
11 Song of praise (6)
13 Lessee (6)
14 Liquid measure (5)
15 Ukrainian capital (4)
17 In case (4)
18 Merit (anag.) (5)
20 Hindu hermitage (6)
21 Carry to excess (6)
24 Rabble (3)
25 Watchful (8)
26 Riled (7)
27 IX (4)

DOWN

2 Sluggish (5)
3 Twaddle (6)
4 Cajole (4)
5 French presidential palace (6)
6 Fish sauce (7)
7 Residence (10)
10 Game played with dice (10)
12 Half-semibreve (5)
13 Cornish cathedral (5)
16 Display (7)
18 Wonder (6)
19 John ——, diarist (6)
22 Quarrel; arrest (3,2)
23 Elderly (4)

2

ACROSS

1 Near (5)
4 Siamese people (5)
10 Bonds (7)
11 Sound (5)
12 Happening (5)
13 Boy's name (7)
15 Lugs (4)
17 Portion (5)
19 Keen (5)
22 Eject (4)
25 Pupil (7)
27 Gigantic Greek god (5)
29 Greenfly (5)
30 Gave off (7)
31 Romany (5)
32 Seats (anag.) (5)

DOWN

2 Lissom (5)
3 Metal alloy (7)
5 Players' cards (5)
6 Mimic (7)
7 Frequently (5)
8 Surrey town (5)
9 Relate (5)
14 Sues (anag.) (4)
16 A vast age (4)
18 Arrogant (7)
20 Achieves (7)
21 Film award (5)
23 Complete (5)
24 Derogatory, malicious (5)
26 Relieves, loosens (5)
28 Name (5)

ACROSS

1 Cancel (6)
7 Husbands (colloq.) (7)
8 Laminated (8)
9 Throb (5)
10 Wanderer (5)
11 Boom (4)
12 Perfect (5)
15 Biblical tower (5)
16 Bumpkin (5)
19 Alone (4)
20 Mantra (5)
21 Respond (5)
22 Memento (8)
23 Ground (7)
24 Vegetables (6)

DOWN

1 Theology (8)
2 Damn lark (anag.) (8)
3 Tendency (5)
4 Sludge (3)
5 Ridiculous (6)
6 Japanese hostess (6)
7 Grief-stricken (11)
9 Bucket (4)
13 Stunt (8)
14 Languid (8)
15 Stain (4)
17 Heeded (6)
18 Accompany (6)
20 Gambol (5)
22 Jest; child (slang) (3)

4

ACROSS

4 President —— Reagan (6)
5 Rock (4)
7 Aerodrome (7)
10 Inner Hebridean isle (5)
11 Himalayan mountain (7)
12 Defect (5)
14 Starry (7)
15 Vietnamese capital (5)
16 Manx capital (7)
20 Austrian composer (5)
21 Americans (7)
22 Manfred ——, pop group (4)
23 Beetle (6)

DOWN

1 Shoot from cover (5)
2 Roar (5)
3 At worst (anag.) (3-4)
4 Mar (4)
6 Annual (6)
8 Applause (7)
9 Triad (7)
10 Iranian city (7)
13 Petroleum jelly (6)
14 Covering with turf (7)
17 Beer (5)
18 Shirk (work) (5)
19 eg Skin of an orange (4)

ACROSS

1 Followed (7)
5 List (5)
8 Bird's comb (5)
9 Ripened (7)
10 Femur (5-4)
12 Spoil (3)
13 Punctual; instigate (6)
14 Unconcern (6)
17 Hot drink (3)
18 Five-pointed star (9)
20 Gourmet (7)
21 Steam-bath (5)
23 Slight colouring (5)
24 Outside (anag.) (7)

DOWN

1 Unspoken (5)
2 Mimic (3)
3 Relish (7)
4 Small plum (6)
5 Tenth part (5)
6 Pressure gauge (9)
7 Old (7)
11 Seclusion (9)
13 Uncomplaining; invalid (7)
15 Despair (anag.) (7)
16 Six-legged creature (6)
18 Short delay (5)
19 Resources (5)
22 Flying saucer (3)

6

ACROSS

1 Sudden short attack (5)
4 Hospital worker (5)
10 Throw away (7)
11 Scrub (5)
12 Terrace (5)
13 Acute (7)
15 Short letter (4)
17 Female fox (5)
19 Elude (5)
22 Give way (4)
25 Stomach (7)
27 Opponent (5)
29 Cured pork (5)
30 Ruled (7)
31 Muslim religion (5)
32 Stalks (5)

DOWN

2 Beginning (5)
3 Mother-of-pearl (7)
5 Unhappy (5)
6 Showed contempt (7)
7 Take into family (5)
8 Own up to (5)
9 Short (5)
14 Require (4)
16 Formerly (4)
18 Charges with crime (7)
20 Jury's decision (7)
21 Jewish teacher (5)
23 Ingress (5)
24 Forest clearing (5)
26 Frenzy (5)
28 Poison (5)

ACROSS

7 District (6)
8 Fires (6)
10 Falls (7)
11 Armistice (5)
12 Somersault (4)
13 Torment (5)
17 Canoe (5)
18 Scoff (4)
22 Sewer (5)
23 Abuse (7)
24 Bivalve (6)
25 Browbeat; Trojan hero (6)

DOWN

1 Mention particularly (7)
2 Humdrum (7)
3 Regular (5)
4 Fish (7)
5 Fake (5)
6 Benefit (5)
9 Retribution (9)
14 Wash (7)
15 Fanatics (7)
16 Cheese (7)
19 Dialect (5)
20 Swamp (5)
21 Monarch (5)

8

ACROSS

1 Stealing from (7)
5 Head cover (4)
7 Entire sum (5)
8 Requite (6)
10 Incite, help (4)
11 eg Colander (8)
13 Tried out (6)
14 Agreement (6)
17 Get a vine (anag.) (8)
19 Let it stand (4)
21 Light chestnut (6)
22 —— acids (5)
23 Among (4)
24 Tidies (7)

DOWN

1 Taking back (10)
2 Troubles (7)
3 Misfortunes (4)
4 eg The inhabitants of Brobdingnag (6)
5 Her chair (anag.) (8)
6 Musical instrument (5)
9 Customs (10)
12 Improved (8)
15 Sketch; general statement (7)
16 King Arthur's burial place (6)
18 Stable-hand (5)
20 Norse epic (4)

ACROSS

1 Mr Punch's dog (4)
4 Flawless (7)
8 Arthurian land (8)
9 Sailor (colloq.) (3)
11 Entertained (6)
13 Austria's capital city (6)
14 Weird (5)
15 *King* —— (film) (4)
17 African republic (4)
18 String instrument (5)
20 Illusory (6)
21 Declare, assert (6)
24 Deuce (3)
25 Got better (8)
26 Send tea (anag.) (4,3)
27 Puppet (4)

DOWN

2 *The Very Thought* ——
(song) (2,3)
3 American (6)
4 Italian city (4)
5 Auld —— (Edinburgh)
(6)
6 European republic (7)
7 Solid earth (5,5)
10 Dull (10)
12 Evil spirit (5)
13 Country house (5)
16 Jumpy (7)
18 Overnight bag (6)
19 Give, provide (6)
22 Perfect (5)
23 Hastened (4)

10

ACROSS

1 City in NW Portugal (Portuguese spelling) (5)
4 Caper (6)
9 Caribbean isle (5)
10 Chief city (7)
11 Aircraft body (7)
12 Phoenician city (5)
14 & 15 Stay hidden (3,3)
16 Little devil (3)
18 Atmosphere (3)
21 Locating system (5)
22 Feeler (7)
23 Slip back (7)
25 Cassava (5)
26 Love-apple (6)
27 In Jan (anag.) (5)

DOWN

1 Largest Malay state (6)
2 Uncordial (anag.) (4-5)
3 Yellow songbird (6)
5 Rest (6)
6 eg Almond, brazil (3)
7 London borough (6)
8 Moved faster (11)
13 —— Republic, WI (9)
17 Biblical mount (6)
18 Impart (anag.) (6)
19 Remain after normal time (4,2)
20 Second largest country (6)
24 Scottish chimney (3)

ACROSS

1 Follows closely (5)
4 Fixing (7)
8 Immature toad (7)
9 Corn (5)
10 Precise (5)
11 Analgesic (7)
13 Large jug (4)
15 Calm (6)
17 Fisherman (6)
20 Competent (4)
22 Antipathy (7)
24 Conjecture (5)
26 Elevate (5)
27 The rate (anag.) (7)
28 Voter (7)
29 Fundamental belief (5)

DOWN

1 Rags (7)
2 Subcontinent (5)
3 Abbreviate (7)
4 Puncture (6)
5 Wanderer (5)
6 First (7)
7 Large farm birds (5)
12 Spoken (4)
14 Feeble (4)
16 Pause to rest (7)
18 Disregard (7)
19 High regard (7)
21 Superior (6)
22 Funereal music (5)
23 Nitre (anag.) (5)
25 Consumed (5)

12

ACROSS

1 Woodland (6)
4 Middle (5)
8 Profundity (5)
9 Works (7)
10 Anxious (7)
11 Relate (4)
12 Viewed (3)
14 Small landmass (4)
15 Moslem prayer leader (4)
18 Male sheep (3)
21 Totals (4)
23 Sticks (7)
25 Receives (7)
26 Cooking stove (5)
27 City manager (5)
28 Proprietors (6)

DOWN

1 Losing colour (6)
2 Makes known (7)
3 Sailing ship (8)
4 Vagrant (4)
5 Blue (5)
6 Fight (6)
7 Sanctify (5)
13 Retreat (8)
16 Put in order (7)
17 Incendiary bomb
ingredient (6)
19 Swamp (5)
20 Rate (6)
22 Lure (5)
24 Egg on (4)

ACROSS

1 Vulgar (6)
7 Angling (7)
8 Infallible (4-4)
9 Shepherd's staff (5)
10 Aimed (anag.) (5)
11 Average level (4)
12 Advantage (5)
15 Indian title (5)
16 Choose (5)
19 Detest (4)
20 Muse of love poetry (5)
21 Hebridean island (5)
22 Church service (8)
23 Reception (7)
24 Hebrew judge (6)

DOWN

1 Fine wool (8)
2 Large terrier (8)
3 Bulgarian capital (5)
4 Compete (3)
5 Amulets; entrances (6)
6 Play it again! (6)
7 Unauthorised absence (6,5)
9 Crustacean (4)
13 Tree (8)
14 Sledge (8)
15 Sojourn (4)
17 Not as great (6)
18 Risk (6)
20 Boredom (5)
22 Flightless bird (3)

14

ACROSS

1 Cooling device (3)
3 Ocean (3)
5 Replete (4)
7 Goes ahead (5)
8 Ill-met (anag.) (6)
10 The Garden of —— (4)
11 Marries (8)
13 Adds up to (6)
14 Italian region (6)
17 Strong sedative drug (8)
19 East European (4)
21 Deed (6)
22 Reef-forming sea life (5)
23 Social insects (4)
24 Norm (3)
25 Age (3)

DOWN

1 Kentish port (10)
2 Rat seen (anag.) (7)
3 Tolerable, indifferent (2-2)
4 Nearly (6)
5 Take a tumble (4,4)
6 Vegetables (5)
9 Birmingham football club (5,5)
12 Acclamations (8)
15 Make bigger (7)
16 Strong-smelling herb (6)
18 French wine region (5)
20 Sign of injury (4)

ACROSS

1 —— Ziegfeld (impresario) (7)
5 End of the day (5)
8 Fireplace nook (5)
9 Military hospital in 19 war (7)
10 Scottish emblem (7)
11 Pakistan river (5)
12 Ministering spirits (6)
14 Hot tar (anag.) (6)
17 *Carry on* —— (film) (5)
19 1853-6 War (7)
22 Dependent (7)
23 Assault (5)
24 Spanish hero (2,3)
25 Constable's wagon (3,4)

DOWN

1 Sparky mineral (5)
2 Continuing (2-5)
3 Happening (5)
4 Orange/lemon peel scraper (6)
5 Feed (7)
6 Great (5)
7 Cardigan and jumper (7)
12 6 National course (7)
13 Drew ale (anag.) (7)
15 Unenclosed ocean (4,3)
16 Frustrate; quash (6)
18 Souvenir (5)
20 Dentine (5)
21 ie Out (3,2)

16

ACROSS

1 Angry (5)
4 Spun (7)
8 Perplexes (7)
9 Shelf (5)
10 Japanese American (5)
11 Implore (7)
13 Scottish isle (4)
15 —— the Divine (2,4)
17 Fungus (6)
20 Monster (4)
22 Ape, wolf (anag.) (7)
24 Fast and neat (5)
26 Swift (5)
27 Sleeping (7)
28 Dutch philosopher (7)
29 Cyril (anag.) (5)

DOWN

1 Cog pins (anag.) (7)
2 Exudes (5)
3 Ungenerous (7)
4 Methodist hymn-writer (6)
5 Small landmass (5)
6 Large cervine animal (3,4)
7 Lived (5)
12 Close (4)
14 Realise (4)
16 Spanish lady's name (7)
18 Not specific (7)
19 Sort of crossword (7)
21 Lady's name (6)
22 Ill-feeling (5)
23 Tarred rope (5)
25 Talent (5)

ACROSS

7 Wave (6)
8 Gazes (6)
10 Remarkable (7)
11 String (5)
12 Past; surplus (4)
13 Hazy (5)
17 Intrepid (5)
18 Mere (4)
22 Representative (5)
23 Zero (7)
24 Sister (anag.) (6)
25 Dive (6)

DOWN

1 Desert (7)
2 Sparkle (7)
3 Uncertainty (5)
4 Set taut (anag.) (7)
5 Characteristic (5)
6 Willow (5)
9 Crediting (9)
14 Objection (7)
15 Uncomplaining; invalid (7)
16 Ruled (7)
19 Hirsute (5)
20 Sumptuous meal (5)
21 Stem; follow (5)

18

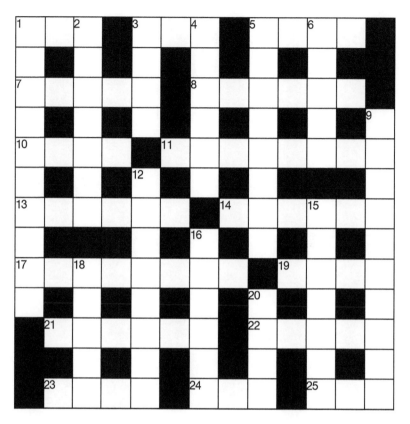

ACROSS

1 Against (3)
3 Not many (3)
5 Jerusalem (4)
7 Junior (5)
8 Retard (anag.) (6)
10 Gospel writer (4)
11 Commotion (8)
13 Confuse (6)
14 Town in Mid-Wales (6)
17 Many (8)
19 Japanese mountain (4)
21 Urge strongly (6)
22 Weed (5)
23 Poisonous tree (4)
24 Male sheep (3)
25 Crimson (3)

DOWN

1 Congratulate (10)
2 Don's kin (anag.) (3-4)
3 Pronged instrument (4)
4 Indoors (6)
5 Extremism (8)
6 Mountain nymph (5)
9 Waved (10)
12 Illustrious (8)
15 Confused mess (7)
16 Professional gambler; client (inf.) (6)
18 Confused jumble (3-2)
20 Egg (4)

ACROSS

1 Cooked by radiant heat (7)
8 Pales (6)
9 Renounced (7)
11 Gods lied (anag.) (8)
12 Unadorned (5)
14 Used to be (4)
15 Decapitated (8)
17 Arterial obstruction (8)
18 Scheme; map (4)
20 Wide-awake (5)
21 Sewage container (8)
23 Nine-sided figure (7)
24 Vanquished (6)
25 Merrymaking (7)

DOWN

2 Refund (6)
3 Parisian museum (6)
4 Ogled (4)
5 Artist's studio (7)
6 Vamoose (9)
7 Rising (9)
10 Alternative route (9)
12 Variety of maize (9)
13 Ballet posture (9)
16 Sailing-ship (7)
18 Asleep (anag.) (6)
19 Bower (6)
22 Only, sole (4)

20

ACROSS

1 Royal mansion (6)
4 Assistants (5)
8 —— Wilde (5)
9 Unyielding (7)
10 Abrasion (7)
11 Ruse (anag.) (4)
12 Drink daintily (3)
14 —— shui (4)
15 Seaweed (4)
18 Before (poetic) (3)
21 Mountain range (4)
23 Dryness (7)
25 A follower of Jesus (7)
26 Japanese warrior (5)
27 Amidst (5)
28 Lord —— , *Telegraph* writer (6)

DOWN

1 For the time being (3,3)
2 Milk sugar (7)
3 Horse-drawn vehicle (8)
4 Woe is me! (4)
5 Faces (5)
6 Stitch up (wound) (6)
7 Lakes (5)
13 Gilbert & Sullivan opera (8)
16 Smiled broadly (7)
17 Country (6)
19 Avid (5)
20 Local regulations (6)
22 Camera picture (5)
24 Male deer (4)

ACROSS

1 Hair restraint (7)
5 Reels (anag.) (5)
8 Wooden shoe (5)
9 Smash to pieces (7)
10 Overweight (9)
12 Decompose (3)
13 Depredator (6)
14 Affix (6)
17 Dry (wine) (3)
18 Forbearance (9)
20 Foliage (7)
21 Dispute (5)
23 Artist's stand (5)
24 Soaked (7)

DOWN

1 Fundamental (5)
2 Seize (3)
3 Show keenness (7)
4 Northern Ireland (6)
5 Smallest (5)
6 Amuse (9)
7 Elongate (7)
11 Croatians (anag.) (9)
13 Determine (7)
15 Row of houses (7)
16 Nippers (6)
18 Follow; path (5)
19 Edit, improve (5)
22 Aperture (3)

22

ACROSS

1 Medical practitioner (7)
5 Group together (5)
8 Macho type (2-3)
9 Student (7)
10 eg Gold bars (7)
11 Correspond (5)
12 Brusque (6)
14 Severe (6)
17 Keen (5)
19 Hangs around (7)
22 High and dry (7)
23 Hurl (5)
24 Roman Eros (5)
25 Sincere (7)

DOWN

1 Former Indian title (5)
2 Walker (7)
3 Boredom (5)
4 Stockings (6)
5 Totally obvious (7)
6 Male singing voice (5)
7 Reap (7)
12 Astringent in tone (7)
13 Very thirsty (7)
15 Make a list (7)
16 Promise (6)
18 Get hold of (5)
20 Deduce (5)
21 Visual perception (5)

ACROSS

1 Spanning (8)
5 Solitary (4)
8 Fine face (anag.) (8)
9 Tumbled (4)
11 Anyway (2,3,6)
14 Fool (3)
16 Bury (5)
17 Always (3)
18 Mensuration (11)
21 —— water (4)
22 Scrawl (8)
24 Police spy (4)
25 Standing still (8)

DOWN

1 Dollar; male deer (4)
2 —— dig (5)
3 Sociable (10)
4 Sister (3)
6 Pacific islands (7)
7 Signed up (8)
10 Supervising (10)
12 Supple (5)
13 Italian cheese (8)
15 Calumny (7)
19 Shinbone (5)
20 Worst (4)
23 eg Leopard (3)

24

ACROSS

1 Grass colour (5)
4 Vegetables (4)
8 Doors, gates (7)
9 Garden pest (5)
10 Irish county (5)
11 Prying person (7)
13 Fern foliage (6)
15 Looked angrily (6)
17 By degrees (7)
20 Stare (anag.) (5)
22 Exposes, begins (5)
23 Hurriedly (2,5)
24 Deer (4)
25 Sieves (5)

DOWN

1 Glisten (5)
2 Predicted from known data (12)
3 Whinnied (7)
4 Posse (anag.) (5)
5 Texan battle (5)
6 —— *Penzance* (Gilbert & Sullivan) (3,7,2)
7 Loved, venerated (6)
12 Grumble; horse (3)
13 Bundle of kindling (6)
14 eg Vichy (3)
16 Coniferous trees (7)
18 Overturned (5)
19 Prone (5)
21 Stairs; paces (5)

ACROSS

1 Cheese (4)
5 *Huckleberry* —— (4)
7 Sales desk (7)
8 Renaissance flute (8)
10 Wicked (4)
12 Sir David —— (film director) (4)
14 Fetch! (8)
16 Red meats (anag.) (8)
17 Pant (4)
18 Forbid (4)
19 Advance (8)
22 Dame Julie —— (7)
23 Lofty (4)
24 Eager (4)

DOWN

1 Ale (4)
2 Resound (4)
3 Killer (8)
4 Agitate (4)
5 Very cold (8)
6 Sir —— Coward (4)
9 Dame Edna —— (7)
11 Buys shares (7)
13 Grand —— (Aintree) (8)
15 Stop deal (anag.) (8)
18 Huge (4)
19 Cricket leg-guards (4)
20 Danger (4)
21 Penn, Bean or O'Casey (4)

ACROSS

7 Smart —— (plural) (6)
8 Power-driven tool (6)
10 Kenneth —— , *Wind in the Willows* author (7)
11 Reigning beauty (5)
12 Narrate (4)
13 Receiver (5)
17 Dizzy (5)
18 Short visit (4)
22 Biblical king (5)
23 Foreign (7)
24 Long prayer (6)
25 Speaking-tube (6)

DOWN

1 Mischievous (7)
2 A failing (7)
3 —— -dhu, dirk (5)
4 Young Italian child (7)
5 Curiously (5)
6 Egret (anag.) (5)
9 Nonconformist (9)
14 Pealing (7)
15 Nocturnal bird (4,3)
16 Branch of mathematics (7)
19 Suggest (5)
20 Onyx (5)
21 Interrogate (5)

ACROSS

1 Culinary herb (5)
4 Disconnected (6)
9 Warlike (7)
10 Cloudiness (5)
11 Otherwise (4)
12 Small country house (7)
13 Tibetan animal (3)
14 Wander (4)
16 Mimicked (4)
18 Drink; circuit (3)
20 Back up (7)
21 Each (anag.) (4)
24 Mediterranean island (5)
25 Relevant (7)
26 Flag (6)
27 Guide (5)

DOWN

1 Wood (6)
2 Stories; threads (5)
3 Egress (4)
5 Patching (anag.) (8)
6 Set apart (7)
7 Moisten (6)
8 Courage (5)
13 Relaying (anag.) (8)
15 —— complex (7)
17 Save (6)
18 Shelf (5)
19 Choose (6)
22 Creep (5)
23 Hold tight (4)

28

ACROSS

1 Undefined number (4)
4 Mount an attack (7)
8 Contravene (8)
9 Mother (3)
11 Tun (6)
13 Exaggerate (6)
14 Dunderhead (5)
15 Lie in wait (4)
17 Hindu ascetic (4)
18 Less (5)
20 In truth (6)
21 Baby's toy (6)
24 Zero (3)
25 Brutal (8)
26 Keenly (7)
27 Repeat (4)

DOWN

2 Possessor (5)
3 Gained (6)
4 Skin disease (4)
5 Postpone (6)
6 Experience (7)
7 Used delaying tactics (10)
10 Exuberance (10)
12 Crystal clear (5)
13 Happen (5)
16 Communist banner (3,4)
18 Associate (6)
19 Ferocious (6)
22 Upper leg (5)
23 Draught horse (4)

ACROSS

1 Couple (4)
4 Moulded (6)
7 Consume (3)
9 Gnarl (4)
10 Stirred (8)
11 Irritate (3)
12 Lean (4)
13 Prevalent disease (8)
16 Racing horse (13)
19 I get a van (anag.) (8)
23 Bellow (4)
24 Low (3)
25 Type of vinegar (8)
26 Pelt (4)
27 Self (3)
28 Snuggle (6)
29 Long and lean (4)

DOWN

2 Shakespeare's wife (4,8)
3 Suite (7)
4 Pale (5)
5 Legal excuse (5)
6 Avoid (5)
8 Consideration (12)
14 Leapt (anag.) (5)
15 Note (3)
17 Farm animal (3)
18 Air-spray (7)
20 Progeny (5)
21 Let in; confess (5)
22 Host (5)

30

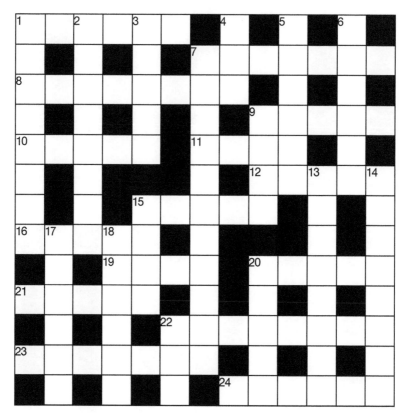

ACROSS

1 Athlete (6)
7 Cecil B —— (films) (2,5)
8 Circle's width (8)
9 Greek S (5)
10 Heraldic device (5)
11 Skinny (4)
12 Legal (5)
15 Unit of weight for gems (5)
16 Treen (anag.) (5)
19 eg A shower (4)
20 Italian wine region (5)
21 Dairy product (5)
22 Gemstone (8)
23 Royal state (7)
24 American city (6)

DOWN

1 Mockery (8)
2 The Balkans and Turkey (4,4)
3 Upright (5)
4 For each (3)
5 Italian resort (6)
6 Ex-students (6)
7 OT book (11)
9 Sediment (4)
13 Agent for change (8)
14 Devon town (8)
15 Stuff (4)
17 Scandinavian state (6)
18 Wiped out (6)
20 Scrap (3-2)
22 Tea (anag.) (3)

ACROSS

1 Former Gold Coast (5)
4 Cleanse (4)
8 *It's —— Again* (WW2 radio show) (4,3)
9 Correct (5)
10 Route (anag.) (5)
11 Mr, Sir (Dutch) (7)
13 Victoria's consort (6)
15 Marsh (6)
17 Huge number (7)
20 Fetch (5)
22 Smart girl (5)
23 Beloved (7)
24 Remain (4)
25 Cairo's country (5)

DOWN

1 Arrive at, reach (3,2)
2 Possibility of being modified (12)
3 Lover (7)
4 You can't —— all! (3,2)
5 Small finch (5)
6 Possibility of concurring (12)
7 Begins (6)
12 Sweet potato (3)
13 New Zealand soldiers (6)
14 1 + 1 (3)
16 13ac's IOW house (7)
18 Clumsy (5)
19 —— and Big Ears (5)
21 Leg of mutton (5)

32

ACROSS

1 *Mal de* —— (3)
3 Speak (3)
5 Ds (4)
7 Oscillate (5)
8 Funeral car (6)
10 Killer-whale (4)
11 Insects' sense-organs (8)
13 Persian kings (6)
14 Hidden (6)
17 Shipwrecked person (8)
19 Duck (4)
21 Skilful (6)
22 Pirate (5)
23 Use needles (4)
24 Motor-coach (3)
25 Circuit (3)

DOWN

1 Bad behaviour (10)
2 Passenger vehicle (7)
3 Wise man (4)
4 Jehovah (6)
5 Racing-car (8)
6 Lease (anag.) (5)
9 Rickety vehicle (10)
12 Small light vehicle (8)
15 Transference (7)
16 Of Cambridge (6)
18 Andes (anag.) (5)
20 Love-god (4)

ACROSS

1 Assembled (8)
7 Yields (5)
8 Paint; animal disease (9)
9 Write (3)
10 Welsh emblem (4)
11 Without delay (6)
13 Putrid (6)
14 Thick soup (6)
17 Superior; gambler (6)
18 Go by (4)
20 Level result (3)
22 Rebel (9)
23 Rule (5)
24 Early spring flower (8)

DOWN

1 Prototype (5)
2 Distrust (7)
3 Regular (4)
4 Run out, exhale (6)
5 Taped (anag.) (5)
6 Foolish (7)
7 Red (7)
12 Sure (7)
13 Exaltation (7)
15 Non-professional (7)
16 Time of year (6)
17 Commence (5)
19 Contrived situation (3-2)
21 Sketch; attraction (4)

34

ACROSS

1 Hit (6)
4 Portion (5)
8 Indeterminate (5)
9 Deliver a talk (7)
10 Obtaining (7)
11 Accomplishment (4)
12 Cosh; plant's juice (3)
14 Silly (4)
15 Bridge span (4)
18 Viewed (3)
21 Rear (4)
23 Stir (7)
25 Go forward (7)
26 Wanderer (5)
27 Gains (5)
28 Supply ship (6)

DOWN

1 Fierce (6)
2 Boat race meeting (7)
3 Apothecaries (8)
4 Dismiss (4)
5 Severe (5)
6 Throws out (6)
7 Droops (5)
13 Forbearance (8)
16 Asserted (7)
17 On fire (6)
19 Gamble (5)
20 Sexual status (6)
22 Enshroud (5)
24 Burden (4)

ACROSS

4 Neigh (6)
5 —— Hoyle, astronomer (4)
7 Incapacitate (7)
10 Fusillade (5)
11 Told; akin (7)
12 Forest clearing (5)
14 Nom-de-plume (3,4)
15 Concise (5)
16 Chinese tonic (7)
20 Be buoyant (5)
21 Bacterial disease (7)
22 Putsch (4)
23 Kind of smoked haddock (6)

DOWN

1 North-east Indian state (5)
2 Funeral-bell (5)
3 Foot-lever (7)
4 Dam (4)
6 Split up (6)
8 Avail (7)
9 Nearest (anag.) (7)
10 Section of a circle (7)
13 Gambol (6)
14 Winged horse (7)
17 Uncanny (5)
18 Haggard (5)
19 Wrecked building (4)

36

ACROSS

1 Undulating (7)
5 Plied the oars (5)
8 Ebbing and flowing (5)
9 Calculate size (7)
10 Kerchief (9)
12 Greek underworld (3)
13 Flying island in *Gulliver's Travels* (6)
14 Courage (6)
17 And not; neither (3)
18 Deserted (9)
20 Very obvious (7)
21 Blusher (5)
23 Odin (5)
24 Tend NCO (anag.) (7)

DOWN

1 Observe; timepiece (5)
2 Signify assent (3)
3 Unlawful (7)
4 Frisk (6)
5 Attain (5)
6 Relaxed after strenuous activity (5,4)
7 Redress (anag.) (7)
11 & (9)
13 Medieval weapon (7)
15 Firedog (7)
16 Northern sea (6)
18 Once more (5)
19 Terrible fear (5)
22 Yorkshire river (3)

ACROSS

1 Merely (4)
4 Colts (5)
8 One dress (anag.) (8)
9 Sure thing (colloq.) (4)
10 Prejudice (4)
11 Maintained firmly (8)
12 Juliet's hometown (6)
14 Ship's steering apparatus (6)
16 Romeo's family name (8)
19 Small valley (4)
20 Wound (4)
21 Card-game (8)
22 Ship's load (5)
23 Loathe (4)

DOWN

2 —— and crannies (5)
3 Talmud study (7)
4 Goes hungry (5)
5 Defendant (7)
6 Merry frolic (5)
7 eg Nine (anag.) (6)
13 Tenth month (7)
14 eg Hock (7)
15 Funeral oration (6)
17 Relating to sight (5)
18 Lizard (5)
19 First appearance (5)

38

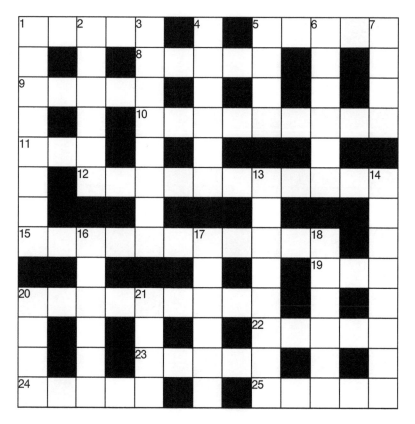

ACROSS

1 Across (prefix) (5)
5 Exhibit publicly; eg soccer (5)
8 Easterner (5)
9 Goblin (5)
10 Formerly (9)
11 Hawaiian garland (3)
12 Nous (11)
15 Releasing (11)
19 Spike of corn (3)
20 It is chewed, not swallowed (6-3)
22 German city (5)
23 European country (5)
24 Appointment (5)
25 3 (5)

DOWN

1 Added together (8)
2 Based on nuclear energy (6)
3 Rep (8)
4 Debacle (6)
5 Frozen flakes (4)
6 Potion (anag.) (6)
7 Kind (4)
13 Consignment (8)
14 Charm (8)
16 New York city trains (6)
17 Person from Jalalabad (6)
18 Hot spring (6)
20 Blemish (4)
21 Inventory (4)

ACROSS

1 Ropes (anag.) (5)
4 Surrender (7)
8 Ingredient (7)
9 Follow (5)
10 Consumed (5)
11 Rapture (7)
13 Counter-tenor (4)
15 Amuse (6)
17 Blabs (6)
20 Run away (4)
22 Chock-a-block (7)
24 Panorama (5)
26 Monk (5)
27 Rushing stream (7)
28 Builder (7)
29 Foe (5)

DOWN

1 Justification, excuse (7)
2 Open (5)
3 Everlasting (7)
4 Chop (6)
5 Appears (5)
6 Second (7)
7 Indigent (5)
12 Manage (4)
14 Departed (4)
16 Overturn (7)
18 Daydream (7)
19 Dark-complexioned (7)
21 eg A, B, C, D (6)
22 Flier (anag.) (5)
23 White heron (5)
25 Scandinavian (5)

ACROSS

1 Compel (5)
4 Hurting (6)
9 Staff restaurant (7)
10 Cuttlefish pigment (5)
11 Lascivious (4)
12 Esteemed (7)
13 Irritate (3)
14 Cash register (4)
16 Reign (4)
18 Primate (3)
20 Put off (7)
21 Young sheep (4)
24 Royal dog (5)
25 Accommodates (7)
26 eg Rat (6)
27 Tear up (5)

DOWN

1 Lacking depth, glibly superficial (6)
2 Renovate (5)
3 Fencing sword (4)
5 Soft wool (8)
6 Endanger (7)
7 Sentries (6)
8 Skulk (5)
13 Magic trick (8)
15 Hurt (7)
17 Ballerina (6)
18 Rile (5)
19 Humbled (6)
22 Foreshadow (5)
23 Regrettably (4)

ACROSS

1 Literary prize (6)
4 Seize forcibly (5)
8 Urgency (5)
9 Sudden pains (7)
10 Mischievous (7)
11 Liberated (4)
12 Health resort (3)
14 Enthusiastic (4)
15 Boring (4)
18 Pull (3)
21 Thought (4)
23 Need (7)
25 Strong emotion (7)
26 Sky blue (5)
27 Verse (5)
28 Erase (6)

DOWN

1 In arrears (6)
2 Little-known (7)
3 Large pachyderm (8)
4 Caprice (4)
5 Keen (5)
6 Tried out (6)
7 Remains (5)
13 Sufficient (8)
16 Free time (7)
17 Smoked herring (6)
19 Incorrect (5)
20 Harsh (6)
22 Attempt (5)
24 Moral weakness (4)

42

ACROSS

1 Wharf (4)
4 Drilled (5)
8 Court of justice (8)
9 Old naval drink (4)
10 Incentive (4)
11 Hinders, shackles (8)
12 Perplex (6)
14 Nailed (anag.) (6)
16 One-storeyed home (8)
19 Bird of prey (4)
20 Arrow; dash (4)
21 French loaf (8)
22 —— Flynn, film star (5)
23 Acting academy (4)

DOWN

2 A brown pigment (5)
3 China's longest river now known as Chang Jiang (7)
4 Light wood (5)
5 Course of treatment (7)
6 Comical (5)
7 Italian brandy (6)
13 Combatant (7)
14 Titled widow (7)
15 Shrewd (6)
17 Treatment (5)
18 Tag (5)
19 Massage (5)

ACROSS

1 Ruler (7)
8 Irish county (6)
9 Examines, views (7)
11 Express boldly (5,3)
12 Bear, tote (5)
14 *Quod —— demonstrandum* (QED) (4)
15 Caviar fish (8)
17 Star fern (anag.) (8)
18 In this place (4)
20 Welfare worker (5)
21 Mimics (8)
23 Perils (7)
24 More noisy (6)
25 Hangs (7)

DOWN

2 Of the eye (6)
3 Refer; commercial (6)
4 Coral islets, eg of the Bahamas (4)
5 Business; amours (7)
6 Pressure gauge (9)
7 Onlooker (9)
10 Trap steed (anag.) (9)
12 Surely (9)
13 Grasping (9)
16 Evaded (7)
18 Bargain (6)
19 Brought up (6)
22 Herb; wise man (4)

44

ACROSS

1 Was clad in (4)
5 Chant (4)
7 William I's wife (7)
8 Australian eucalyptus (8)
10 Forbidden (4)
12 Pal (4)
14 Unbecoming (5,3)
16 Cornish castle (8)
17 Paradise (4)
18 —— *Karenina* (lit.) 4)
19 Precedent-setter (4,4)
22 Can bite (anag.) (7)
23 Fairytale giant (4)
24 March carrying heavy equipment (military sl.) (4)

DOWN

1 Women's army corps (abbrev.) (4)
2 —— Zatopek (runner) (4)
3 Rooms for horses (8)
4 Aspersion (4)
5 —— City in Utah (4,4)
6 Mentor (4)
9 Speech (7)
11 Barnum & —— Circus (7)
13 Fill with delight (8)
15 eg *Greensleeves* (4,4)
18 Florence's river (4)
19 Punch's dog (4)
20 Large town (4)
21 Wyatt —— (US marshal) (4)

45

ACROSS

1 Bats (8)
5 Harbour (4)
8 Formation (8)
9 Greek portico (4)
11 Feathered cork in badminton (11)
14 Mongrel (3)
16 Spartan serf (5)
17 Self (3)
18 Court suspension (11)
21 Seethe (4)
22 Country in southern Africa (8)
24 Yet (4)
25 Tie (4-4)

DOWN

1 Scrum (4)
2 Board game (5)
3 Dishonest, lying (10)
4 Duo (3)
6 Consequence (7)
7 Ta (5,3)
10 Pamper (10)
12 Claw (5)
13 Word-game (8)
15 Exult (7)
19 Bleat (anag.) (5)
20 Biblical passage (4)
23 Rage (3)

46

ACROSS

1 Ill-feeling; fabric (5)
4 Pawns (5)
10 Exact (7)
11 Cleat (anag.) (5)
12 Inuit dwelling (5)
13 Euphoria (7)
15 Went mounted (4)
17 Article (5)
19 Saying (5)
22 Excellent; uncommon (4)
25 Administrator (7)
27 Permit (5)
29 Office workers (5)
30 Late (7)
31 Viper (5)
32 Prone; untruthful (5)

DOWN

2 Perfect (5)
3 Fabulous animal (7)
5 Last Greek letter (5)
6 Deadly; funny (7)
7 Ruin (5)
8 Cross (5)
9 Restrict growth (5)
14 Shakespearean king (4)
16 Monster (4)
18 Parliamentary record (7)
20 Yearned (anag.) (7)
21 Collect (5)
23 Pointer; weapon (5)
24 Possessor (5)
26 Social blunder (5)
28 Burdened (5)

ACROSS

4 Tenders (6)
5 Young urchin (4)
7 Recover humour (5,2)
10 Go in (5)
11 Go over again (7)
12 Nation (5)
14 Allows (7)
15 Beautiful girl (5)
16 A sudden desire (7)
20 False name (5)
21 Lay poem (anag.) (7)
22 Masculine (4)
23 South American cowboy (6)

DOWN

1 Subsequent to (5)
2 Freshwater fish (5)
3 Young swans (7)
4 The mark at darts (4)
6 Constructs (6)
8 Buys back (7)
9 Insurance payment (7)
10 Joy (7)
13 Pandemonium (6)
14 Flexible (7)
17 Bolivian capital (2,3)
18 Geological time period (5)
19 As well (4)

48

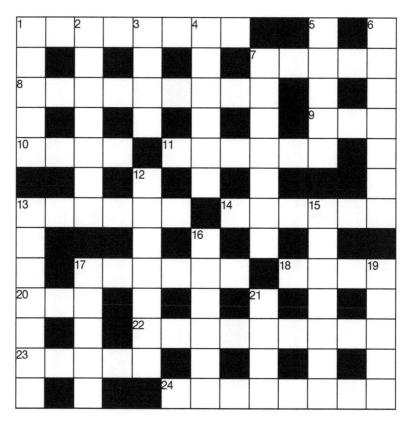

ACROSS

1 White vestment (8)
7 Reputation; shares (5)
8 Imperious (9)
9 Fitting (3)
10 Whirlpool (4)
11 Armed dining chair (6)
13 Celtic language (6)
14 Muscular (6)
17 Beer tap (6)
18 Grasp (4)
20 Still; however (3)
22 Grease (9)
23 Elevate (5)
24 That's Ely (anag.) (8)

DOWN

1 WW1 battlefield (5)
2 Remainder (7)
3 Ogle (4)
4 Middle-Eastern long dress (6)
5 Of the sun (5)
6 Barely outlined (7)
7 Bondage (7)
12 Ludicrous (7)
13 Swiss cheese (7)
15 Authorise, justify (7)
16 Warfare (6)
17 Dye (5)
19 Short and sweet (5)
21 Latvian capital (4)

ACROSS

1 In here (anag.) (6)
4 Of them (5)
8 Savoury jelly (5)
9 East European (7)
10 Made certain of (7)
11 Roman tyrant (4)
12 Decline (3)
14 Dry, withered (4)
15 Eject (4)
18 Pluto (3)
21 Smooth-tongued (4)
23 Frankness (7)
25 The USA (7)
26 Additional (5)
27 Name (5)
28 Stage whispers (6)

DOWN

1 Paradise (6)
2 Witty retort (7)
3 Run cider (anag.) (8)
4 Assignment (4)
5 Banishment (5)
6 Haphazard (6)
7 Wear away (5)
13 Nightclub guards (8)
16 Caught sight of (7)
17 Appalled (6)
19 Fragment (5)
20 Ruptures (6)
22 Passive (5)
24 Heap (4)

50

ACROSS

1 1 (3)
3 Drink (3)
5 —— Blackman (actor) (5)
8 Herb (5)
9 Young dogs (7)
10 Manger (4)
11 Reel sets (anag.) (8)
13 Road convexity (6)
14 Card suit (6)
17 Jewels (8)
19 Sea duck (4)
22 Abates (7)
23 Tale (5)
24 Over-sentimental (5)
25 —— Bevan (NHS) (3)
26 Vast age (3)

DOWN

1 Pub measure (5)
2 Abode of the blessed dead (7)
3 Egyptian canal (4)
4 Documents (6)
5 Occurred (8)
6 Din (5)
7 Sisters (anag.) (7)
12 Retrieval (8)
13 Hugs (7)
15 John Mortimer's —— *of the Bailey* (7)
16 US inventor (6)
18 Fabulist (5)
20 Entrance (3,2)
21 eg Man, Dogs (4)

ACROSS

1 Entrance (4)
4 Cathedral city (7)
8 Dorset resort (8)
9 Ma (3)
11 Macaque (6)
13 Former Spanish currency (6)
14 Remained valid (5)
15 & 17 Isle in Dorset (8)
18 Wobbly food (5)
20 Autographed (6)
21 Church festival (6)
24 Newt (3)
25 Dorset town (8)
26 Dorset resort (7)
27 Cold and damp (4)

DOWN

2 Fat (5)
3 Uproar (6)
4 Hint (4)
5 Resounded (6)
6 Painting medium (7)
7 Disarm rear (anag.) (3-7)
10 Bias favourably (10)
12 Horse (5)
13 Dorset resort (5)
16 Yachting gala (7)
18 Desert rodent (6)
19 Yelped (6)
22 Italian city (5)
23 Vino (4)

52

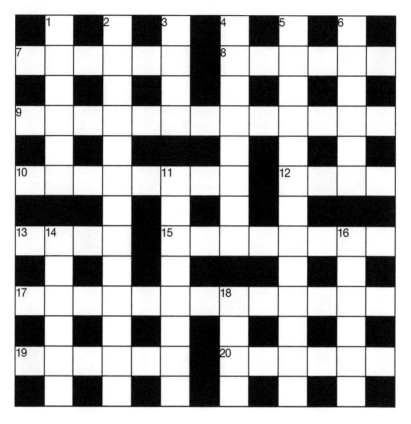

ACROSS

7 Cheshire peninsula (6)
8 Cuba capital (6)
9 Midyear break (6,7)
10 Neolithic (5,3)
12 Performs (4)
13 In the same place (L) (4)
15 Languid (8)
17 —— feeling; disinclination to work (6,7)
19 Courageous (6)
20 Respond (6)

DOWN

1 Slow, graceful dance (6)
2 Ship's passenger amenity (9-4)
3 Aspersion (4)
4 Guns (sl.) (8)
5 Enviable Salsa (anag.) (13)
6 Unimpaired (6)
11 —— and Betty Martin (= nonsense) (3,2,3)
14 Umbrella (colloq.) (6)
16 Day's end (6)
18 Argyll seaport (4)

ACROSS

4 Tasks (6)
5 Shove (4)
7 Had a high opinion of (7)
10 Unwind (5)
11 Convey (7)
12 Creator (5)
14 Overall (7)
15 Sovereign (5)
16 Flavours (7)
20 Draft (5)
21 Oriental (7)
22 Alert (4)
23 Sight (6)

DOWN

1 Hard; three dimensional (5)
2 Gem (5)
3 Burial service (7)
4 Cipher (4)
6 Paradise (6)
8 Judge (7)
9 Illness (7)
10 Stays (7)
13 Tunnel; animal shelter (6)
14 Signal (7)
17 Fertile spot (5)
18 Undress (5)
19 Press (4)

54

ACROSS

1 Lethal (6)
4 Alarm-bell (6)
7 Anodyne (9)
9 Pelt; conceal (4)
10 Pious talk (4)
11 Gripe (5)
13 Lea (6)
14 RE private (6)
15 Summary (6)
17 14-line poem (6)
19 Expiate (5)
20 Anti-aircraft fire (4)
22 Seaweed (4)
23 Mar famine (anag.) (9)
24 Esoteric (6)
25 Doze (6)

DOWN

1 NE English city (6)
2 Swindled (4)
3 Primary colour (6)
4 Dissertation (6)
5 Elegant (4)
6 Gossip (6)
7 Disgustingly (2,7)
8 Bell-tower (9)
11 Punctuation mark (5)
12 Ocean (anag.) (5)
15 Mend one's ways (6)
16 Racial (6)
17 Trapped (6)
18 Hypnotic state (6)
21 German philosopher (4)
22 eg Bullets, shells (4)

56

ACROSS

1 Alien (7)
5 Barmy (4)
7 Detach (5)
8 Announce; gunshot (6)
10 Clammy (4)
11 Pasta (8)
13 Quake (6)
14 Bowdlerise (6)
17 Barrier (8)
19 Disorder (4)
21 Coax (6)
22 Failure (5)
23 Quip (4)
24 Deluge (7)

DOWN

1 Base (10)
2 Entourage (7)
3 Concept (4)
4 Usual (6)
5 Corrupt (8)
6 Waive (5)
9 Contempt (10)
12 Singer (8)
15 Spire (7)
16 Customer (6)
18 Char (5)
20 Insult (4)

ACROSS

1 Lobbies (8)
7 Spill (5)
8 Call, ring (9)
9 Mountain pass (3)
10 Listen to (4)
11 Bequest (6)
13 SOS (6)
14 Abundance (6)
17 Money (sl.) (6)
18 Shod (anag.) (4)
20 Age (3)
22 Paragon (4,5)
23 French coins and notes (5)
24 Keep calm! (6,2)

DOWN

1 Breed (5)
2 Cradle-song (7)
3 Cancel (tape) (4)
4 —— of the Guard (Gilbert & Sullivan) (6)
5 Piquant (5)
6 Shopping vehicle (7)
7 Late Ben (anag.) (7)
12 German tanks (7)
13 Well-off (7)
15 Meridional (7)
16 Charm (6)
17 Wed (5)
19 —— Mirren (actor) (5)
21 Austen novel (4)

58

ACROSS

1 Enter (2,2)
4 Fade (6)
7 Self (3)
9 Jacob's son (OT) (4)
10 Revolution (8)
11 Drink; child (3)
12 Desire (4)
13 Gaiety (8)
16 Counter-charge (13)
19 Plea (8)
23 Restrain (4)
24 Vex (3)
25 Kiss (8)
26 Idle (anag.) (4)
27 Shelter (3)
28 Astute (6)
29 Nimble (4)

DOWN

2 Partiality (3-9)
3 In three (anag.) (7)
4 Value (5)
5 Whole (5)
6 Type of apple (5)
8 Amateur home improvements (2-2-8)
14 Fool (5)
15 Turkish commander (3)
17 Skating surface (3)
18 Grappled with (7)
20 Jagged (5)
21 Startle (5)
22 Relinquish (5)

ACROSS

1 Paint (6)
4 Disconnect; release (5)
8 Wash (5)
9 Supervise (7)
10 Clipped (7)
11 Kind, model (4)
12 Every one (3)
14 Irritate (4)
15 Press; drive (4)
18 Undermine; fool (3)
21 Talk (4)
23 Hermit (7)
25 Stretchy (7)
26 Burning coal (5)
27 Hazy (5)
28 Mean; aim (6)

DOWN

1 Cherry-red (6)
2 Tolerant (7)
3 Sun-hater (anag.) (8)
4 Second-hand (4)
5 Irascible (5)
6 Soccer team (6)
7 Dutch cheese (5)
13 Midday meal (8)
16 Express dissatisfaction (7)
17 Shriek (6)
19 Cost (5)
20 Approached (6)
22 Gather together (5)
24 Remain; support (4)

60

ACROSS

1 Poem (3)
3 Hearing organ (3)
5 Steam engine inventor (4)
7 Sweets in America (5)
8 Affair (6)
10 —— Daniels & Ben Lyon (50s TV) (4)
11 Brave (8)
13 Pact (6)
14 Tell (6)
17 Assess (8)
19 Incline (4)
21 Demur (6)
22 Astound (5)
23 —— of Lochalsh (4)
24 Health resort (3)
25 Fib (3)

DOWN

1 " —— —— twice shy" (4,6)
2 Elevate in rank (7)
3 Etymology (abbrev.) (4)
4 Gypsy (6)
5 Great win (anag.) (8)
6 Tether (3,2)
9 First couple (4,3,3)
12 Mad rush (8)
15 Protective coat (7)
16 Importance, standing (6)
18 Plump (5)
20 Computer language; island (4)

ACROSS

1 Musical note (3)
3 View (3)
5 Moistened flour (5)
8 Skid (5)
9 French West Indian 20 (7)
10 Submit (4)
11 Spanish 20 (8)
13 20 back-to-back (4-2)
14 Need FA (anag.) (6)
17 Ratification (8)
19 Felled (4)
22 Old French 20 (7)
23 Moses's brother (5)
24 Lacking resonance (5)
25 Afflict (3)
26 Foot digit (3)

DOWN

1 20 club (5)
2 Inheritrix (7)
3 Second half of quick 20? (4)
4 Mummify (6)
5 Unstuck (8)
6 Association (5)
7 Square 20 (7)
12 Dexterously (8)
13 Current of air (7)
15 Ballroom 20 (7)
16 Ballroom 20 (6)
18 Slow formal 20 (5)
20 Caned (anag.) (5)
21 20 (4)

62

ACROSS

7 Damage (6)
8 Concept (6)
10 Parcel (7)
11 Frighten (5)
12 Afresh (4)
13 Ghost (5)
17 Stockpile (5)
18 Cried (4)
22 Transparent (5)
23 Sleeping (7)
24 Wild ass (6)
25 Restore; go (6)

DOWN

1 Show (7)
2 Expelled (7)
3 Shatter; respite (5)
4 Giver (7)
5 Essential (5)
6 Antagonist (5)
9 Road speed (anag.) (9)
14 Epicure (7)
15 Escape (7)
16 Height (7)
19 Croat (anag.) (5)
20 Licit (5)
21 Instruction (5)

ACROSS

1 Measure (5)
4 String (5)
10 Intention (7)
11 Barcelona architect (5)
12 Pale-faced (5)
13 Operate (7)
15 Profound (4)
17 Light wood (5)
19 Too soon (5)
22 Grains of rock (4)
25 Modified (7)
27 Pathogen (5)
29 One of the fingers (5)
30 Dishonourable (7)
31 Fatuous (5)
32 Stop (5)

DOWN

2 Soil (5)
3 Reasons (7)
5 Cart (5)
6 Not taking sides (7)
7 Horrify (5)
8 Palisade (5)
9 Crams, packs (5)
14 Overt (4)
16 Facility (4)
18 Desert (7)
20 Bring forward (7)
21 Wooden shack (5)
23 Confess (5)
24 Requested (5)
26 Poison (5)
28 Gowns (5)

64

ACROSS

1 Hawaiian garland (3)
3 Sermoniser (8)
9 Of the kidneys (5)
10 Turn into stone (7)
11 Broadcast; mien (3)
13 Discharge (9)
14 Exotic flower (6)
16 Truth (6)
18 Vain (9)
20 Plastic container (3)
22 One who cowers (7)
23 John ——, explorer (5)
25 Fodder crop (3,5)
26 Cambridgeshire diocese (3)

DOWN

1 eg Caterpillar (5)
2 Hostelry (3)
4 Tapers (anag.) (6)
5 Fred ——, dancer (7)
6 Penitential garment (4,5)
7 Sovereignty (7)
8 Walk heavily (4)
12 Solitary (9)
14 Policeman (7)
15 Whole number (7)
17 Brides (anag.) (6)
19 Large bag (4)
21 Crazy (sl.) (5)
24 Valediction (3)

ACROSS

1 Era (anag.) (3)
3 Pike-like fish (3)
5 Norse epic (4)
7 Subject; melody (5)
8 Jim Henson puppet (6)
10 Pleased (4)
11 Alienate (8)
13 Adds up to (6)
14 Smother (6)
17 Retired professor title (8)
19 Spoilt child (4)
21 Of Cambridge (6)
22 Disney's fawn (5)
23 Rip (4)
24 Insect (3)
25 Religious woman (3)

DOWN

1 Completely (10)
2 Chic (7)
3 Scottish valley (4)
4 Neglectful (6)
5 Divide (8)
6 Eco-friendly (5)
9 Walker (10)
12 Monastery's arcaded walk (8)
15 Name fir (anag.) (7)
16 Din (6)
18 Dodge (5)
20 Competent (4)

66

ACROSS

1 Aberdeen's river (3)
3 Periodical (abbrev.) (3)
5 Smelly (sl.) (5)
8 Odour (5)
9 Rum cake (7)
10 Yin and —— (4)
11 Lingo (8)
13 Projectile (6)
14 Tramples (6)
17 Youth (5,3)
19 Water (L) (4)
22 Crazy people (sl.) (7)
23 Perfect (5)
24 Arrest (3,2)
25 Silent (3)
26 Novel (3)

DOWN

1 Good-looking (colloq.) (5)
2 Ceaseless (7)
3 Dumb (4)
4 —— Holst (music) (6)
5 Direct a ship (8)
6 *Pro* —— (5)
7 New York suburb (7)
12 Marine colour (3-5)
13 Yul —— , actor (7)
15 Steve —— , Hollywood actor (7)
16 Redeem (6)
18 West Ham's Park (5)
20 Permit (5)
21 Motion picture (4)

ACROSS

1 Scottish resort (3)
3 Obvious (8)
9 Early (anag.) (5)
10 From cause to effect (Latin) (1,6)
11 Astern (3)
13 Scottish airport (9)
14 Scottish resort (6)
16 Notify (6)
18 Town on Mull (9)
20 Bumped into (3)
22 Middle Easterner (7)
23 Cattle round-up (5)
25 Chief element (8)
26 Spirit (3)

DOWN

1 Town near Stirling (5)
2 Flatfish (3)
4 Heavenly body (6)
5 Ventilated (7)
6 Amorous temperament (9)
7 Slow flow (7)
8 Harvest (4)
12 Scottish golf-course (9)
14 West Sussex airport (7)
15 Breeziest (7)
17 Salve (6)
19 Walled city (4)
21 Scottish golf-course (5)
24 Delve (3)

68

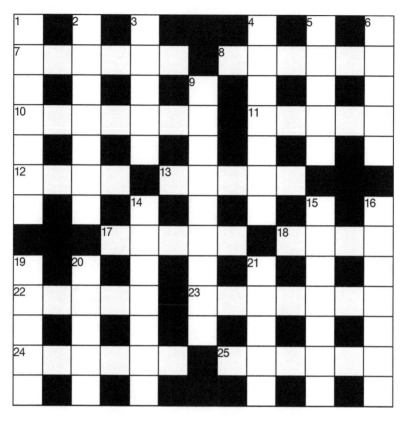

ACROSS

7 Voyage (6)
8 Prophetesses (6)
10 Beaming (7)
11 Discrimination (5)
12 Diminutive (4)
13 Smashed (5)
17 Name (5)
18 Influence; draw (4)
22 Step (5)
23 Height (7)
24 Stringed instrument (6)
25 Ripe (6)

DOWN

1 Care etc. (anag.) (7)
2 Sweet course (7)
3 Try; writing (5)
4 Error (7)
5 Romany (5)
6 Enquired; invited (5)
9 Disinfect (9)
14 Contempt (7)
15 Burial mound (7)
16 Changed (7)
19 Cooker (5)
20 Beneath (5)
21 Man-made waterway (5)

ACROSS

1 Garden tool (4)
4 Viking name for York (6)
7 Low (of cattle) (3)
9 Axe (4)
10 Devastate (3,5)
11 Decompose (3)
12 Yield (4)
13 Joined metals (8)
16 Australian state (3,5,5)
19 A lover's song (8)
23 Trick (4)
24 Knock sharply (3)
25 More exotic (8)
26 Burden (4)
27 Rower (3)
28 Annoy persistently (6)
29 Roman garment (4)

DOWN

2 Accomplishments (12)
3 Female ruler (7)
4 Jostles; shocks (5)
5 Regal (5)
6 Angry (5)
8 Russian city (2,10)
14 Chose (5)
15 Morning moisture (3)
17 Possess (3)
18 Terminal for planes (7)
20 Rub out (5)
21 Anguish (5)
22 Mistake (5)

70

ACROSS

1 Tempus —— (5)
5 Quarrels (5)
8 Soil (5)
9 Inamorato (5)
10 Rover (9)
11 Possess (3)
12 Jumping insect (11)
15 Golden mean (5,6)
19 Chopper (3)
20 Recommends (9)
22 Middle-ear bone (5)
23 Tropical lizard (5)
24 Burly (5)
25 Of birth (5)

DOWN

1 Cornish resort (8)
2 Granting (6)
3 Try a rite (anag.) (8)
4 Tribulations (6)
5 You (archaic) (4)
6 Stimulus (6)
7 Prophet (4)
13 Exclusion (8)
14 Setback (8)
16 Stately dance (6)
17 Lure (6)
18 Lucky charm (6)
20 Jezebel's husband (4)
21 Secretive (4)

ACROSS

1 Perfume (5)
4 Slab for lawn (4)
7 Cargo space (4)
8 Old cavalry volunteer force (8)
9 Prehistoric period (6,3)
10 & 16 Very nearly (3,3)
12 Turn upside down (6)
14 Hurled (6)
16 See 10
18 Holy city (9)
21 Like a Cervantes character (8)
22 Part of shoe (4)
23 Old instrument (4)
24 Made a mistake (5)

DOWN

1 Highlander's pouch (7)
2 Imperil (8)
3 Herb (5)
4 Hard wood (4)
5 Of the countryside (5)
6 Battled (6)
11 Short rest (8)
13 Agreement between nations (6)
15 Saturday and Sunday (7)
17 Charging of excessive interest (5)
19 Male family member (5)
20 Rod between wheels (4)

72

ACROSS

1 Festive occasion (7)
5 Autumn in America (4)
7 —— *So Vain* (song) (3'2)
8 Rang a bell (6)
10 Lily (4)
11 Me on road (anag.) (8)
13 Young cat (6)
14 Dog-house (6)
17 Room warmer (8)
19 Small and sweet (4)
21 Skylight (6)
22 Fragrance (5)
23 Slip (4)
24 Rabbie Burns's wee mouse (7)

DOWN

1 Careless pedestrians (10)
2 Wine perfume (7)
3 Welsh emblem (4)
4 Crowd scene actors (6)
5 Tumbled (4,4)
6 Get up late (3,2)
9 Water down (10)
12 Looked at (8)
15 ——, IOW or RI (7)
16 Spider's net (6)
18 Tipple (5)
20 So long! (2-2)

ACROSS

1 Hum (4)
5 Busy insects (4)
7 Investigate (7)
8 Obstruction (8)
10 Deathly pale (4)
12 Poke (4)
14 Virility (8)
16 Retrains (anag.) (8)
17 Maggot (4)
18 Young deer (4)
19 Guide's fee (8)
22 Hat (7)
23 Bird of prey (4)
24 —— *fortis* (4)

DOWN

1 Vivacity (4)
2 Enthusiasm (4)
3 Woman's lover (colloq.) (5,3)
4 Jazz dance (4)
5 Conducting oneself (8)
6 Influence (4)
9 Hat (7)
11 Hat (7)
13 Agonised (anag.) (8)
15 Negligent (8)
18 Criticism (colloq.) (4)
19 Jetty (4)
20 Large sea-fish (4)
21 Italian isle (4)

74

ACROSS

1 Get into line (5)
4 Heaviness (6)
9 Greed (7)
10 Foxiness (5)
11 Female sheep (4)
12 Even (7)
13 Attempt (3)
14 Operatic song (4)
16 Naked (4)
18 Follow; pet (3)
20 Keep back (7)
21 Post; armour (4)
24 Hold tight (5)
25 Quicker (7)
26 Very thin (6)
27 Greet (anag.) (5)

DOWN

1 Tremble; note (6)
2 Expunge (5)
3 Wicked (4)
5 Delightful; promising (8)
6 Cooked; questioned (7)
7 Hypothesis (6)
8 Very tired (5)
13 Culinary herb (8)
15 Italian composer (7)
17 Splits; quips (6)
18 Thick (5)
19 Bordeaux (6)
22 Thespian (5)
23 Dreadful (4)

ACROSS

1 Digit (5)
4 Fools (5)
10 Permission (7)
11 Not heavy (5)
12 Distressed (5)
13 Mild (7)
15 Reverberation (4)
17 Very steep (5)
19 Read (5)
22 Profanity (4)
25 Arm muscle (7)
27 Relative proportion (5)
29 Engine (5)
30 Joy (7)
31 Love (5)
32 Whispered comment (5)

DOWN

2 Poor writers (5)
3 Sea cow (7)
5 Figure out (5)
6 Boffin (7)
7 Defy (5)
8 Instruct (5)
9 Assert (5)
14 Mislaid (4)
16 Harvest (4)
18 Lifted (7)
20 Menaces (7)
21 Baffle (5)
23 Requested (5)
24 Knoll (5)
26 Mistake (5)
28 Sampled (5)

76

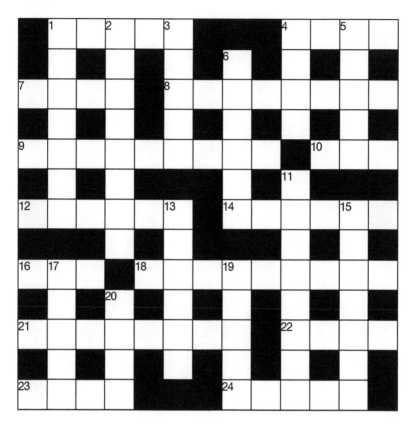

ACROSS

1 Wrench away (5)
4 Sated (4)
7 Telephone (4)
8 Final stop (8)
9 Stupidity (9)
10 Stain (3)
12 Sick (6)
14 Vivacious (6)
16 Hedera (3)
18 Basic matter (9)
21 Dan Green (anag.) (8)
22 Breach (4)
23 Nuisance (4)
24 Pugilist (5)

DOWN

1 Pentecost (7)
2 Give rise to (8)
3 Old giant (5)
4 Let down (4)
5 Verminous (5)
6 Vicious (6)
11 eg Amy Johnson (8)
13 Loll about (6)
15 Morning star (7)
17 Meeting-place (5)
19 Brushwood (5)
20 Throw; mould (4)

ACROSS

1 Skin growths (5)
4 Malay skirt (6)
9 Thrash (7)
10 Trace (anag.) (5)
11 Ingests (4)
12 Clear (7)
13 Din; line (3)
14 Chum (4)
16 —— the Lioness (4)
18 WWII women's auxiliary (3)
20 Swell (7)
21 Roman robe (4)
24 Northern Ireland port (5)
25 Avert, hinder (7)
26 Give (6)
27 Adhesive (5)

DOWN

1 Purse for notes (6)
2 Send (money) (5)
3 Fake (4)
5 Records (8)
6 Retail branches (7)
7 Spin (6)
8 Scatter (5)
13 Deeply respectful (8)
15 Unplaced racehorse (4-3)
17 Dad led (anag.) (6)
18 Skilful (5)
19 Cows, steers (6)
22 Portents (5)
23 Retain (4)

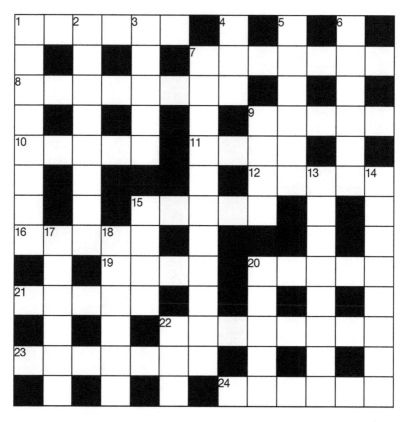

ACROSS

1 Verse metre (6)
7 Noise from closed lips (7)
8 Val's need (anag.) (8)
9 American marshy delta (5)
10 Weird (5)
11 Costly (4)
12 Secret store (5)
15 Bumptious (5)
16 Rope fibre (5)
19 p. (mus.) (4)
20 Tied up (5)
21 Spar (5)
22 Main character in *The Tempest* (8)
23 Delights (7)
24 —— *Spirit* (play) (6)

DOWN

1 Arctic sea hazards (8)
2 Schoolteacher (8)
3 Furious (5)
4 Failure (3)
5 Tell (6)
6 Pries (6)
7 Rest ashamed (anag.) (11)
9 Party (colloq.) (4)
13 Dispute (8)
14 Good-looking (8)
15 Blemish (4)
17 Frozen water drops (6)
18 Dressed stone (6)
20 Mr Fawlty (5)
22 Female swan (3)

ACROSS

4 Speak with another (6)
5 Watch TV (4)
7 Cor —— (musical instrument) (7)
10 Literary style (5)
11 Single amount of money (4,3)
12 Abundant (5)
14 Italian woman (7)
15 Small particle (5)
16 Senior citizen (7)
20 Join (5)
21 Pleasure-seeking (7)
22 Part of the foot (4)
23 European language (6)

DOWN

1 Interrogate (5)
2 Cotton fabric (5)
3 Problem (7)
4 Small horse (4)
6 Trill (6)
8 Capable of being heard (7)
9 European language (7)
10 Protected (7)
13 European language (6)
14 Thermos (anag.) (7)
17 Doctrine (5)
18 Spacious (5)
19 Leo (4)

80

ACROSS

1 Author of *Cakes and Ale* (7)
5 French Impressionist (5)
8 More mature (5)
9 Cinders (anag.) (7)
10 Everlasting (7)
11 Passageway (5)
12 Complete (6)
14 Empty (6)
17 Concur (5)
19 Smart (7)
22 Dry white wine (7)
23 Once more (5)
24 Trench (5)
25 Wraith (7)

DOWN

1 Combine (5)
2 Very many (7)
3 Wading bird (5)
4 Centre (6)
5 Eye makeup (7)
6 Requires (5)
7 Touching line (7)
12 Limp (7)
13 The last (anag.) (7)
15 Obdurate (7)
16 Head-count (6)
18 Oven-cook (5)
20 Expunge (5)
21 Metric weight (5)

ACROSS

7 Heaviness (6)
8 Planet (6)
10 Mental distress (7)
11 Greek island (5)
12 Greek god of love (4)
13 Counterfeit (5)
17 Native New Zealander (5)
18 Eye infection (4)
22 Western Australia's capital (5)
23 King Arthur's capital (7)
24 Maria — , opera singer (6)
25 French impressionist (6)

DOWN

1 Jersey (7)
2 Realm (7)
3 Professorship (5)
4 Roman god of wine (7)
5 Indian currency (5)
6 South American mountains (5)
9 Rule by clergy (9)
14 Capital of Iraq (7)
15 Blue cheese (7)
16 News agency (7)
19 Emptiness (5)
20 Scandinavian monster (5)
21 Yellow resin (5)

82

ACROSS

1 Foolish (5)
4 Lassie (anag.) (6)
9 Hit flaw (anag.) (7)
10 French impressionist (5)
11 Type of agate (4)
12 Threadwork (7)
13 Tear (3)
14 Die away (4)
16 Naked (4)
18 Junk; make lace (3)
20 Arrogance (7)
21 Greek cheese (4)
24 Square-bashing (5)
25 Shoulder blade (7)
26 Judged (6)
27 Two-footed animal (5)

DOWN

1 Educate (6)
2 Cash (5)
3 Gape (4)
5 Risqué (8)
6 Loiterer (7)
7 Nun (6)
8 Baffle (5)
13 Waking signal (8)
15 Insulting (7)
17 Rebuked (6)
18 Lovers' meeting (5)
19 Danger (6)
22 Furnish (5)
23 Gibe (4)

ACROSS

1 Reserved (6)
4 Made from acorn's tree (5)
8 Sorrow (5)
9 Straggler (7)
10 Devon resort (7)
11 Abated (4)
12 Witnessed (3)
14 Not pro (4)
15 Protuberance (4)
18 Donkey (3)
21 Sort (4)
23 French painter (7)
25 Dictionary (7)
26 English poet (5)
27 Ecologically correct (5)
28 Pre-Christmas period (6)

DOWN

1 Capital of Colombia (6)
2 Greek letter (7)
3 Nasty smells (8)
4 Wild party (4)
5 Jack in the pack (5)
6 Small swelling (6)
7 Dramatic works (5)
13 Young expert (5-3)
16 Authorisation (7)
17 POW camp (6)
19 Tea-time treat (5)
20 Rich travellers (3,3)
22 Creature like fairy or elf (5)
24 Examine closely (4)

84

ACROSS

7 Seven —— for Seven Brothers (film) (6)
8 Pat —— (jockey) (6)
10 Went to see (7)
11 Tropical fruit (5)
12 Employed (4)
13 Exclusive news story (5)
17 Corrodes (5)
18 Gas; light (4)
22 Submarine detection device (5)
23 Cute moo (anag.) (7)
24 Oily (6)
25 & 19 Vile Bodies novelist (6, 5)

DOWN

1 —— the Waves (WW2 film) (5,2)
2 eg York (7)
3 Open country (5)
4 Born Free writer (7)
5 Wren, Lind etc(5)
6 Don Juan poet (5)
9 A tonic due (anag.) (9)
14 Achievement (7)
15 Retread (7)
16 Hell for Dante (7)
19 See 25
20 Time waster (5)
21 Sir —— Redgrave (oarsman) (5)

ACROSS

1 Pliant twig, osier (6)
7 Spun (7)
8 Medicinal (8)
9 Esau's brother (5)
10 Suitor (5)
11 Futile (4)
12 Hinge (anag.) (5)
15 Garden flower (5)
16 River transport (5)
19 At first; formerly (4)
20 Pansy genus (5)
21 Cunning (5)
22 Snowstorm (8)
23 Height (7)
24 Blood-vessel (6)

DOWN

1 Lycanthrope (8)
2 Not a nobleman (8)
3 Sea-duck (5)
4 Pointed instrument (3)
5 Mysterious (6)
6 Appertain (6)
7 Smelling-salts (3,8)
9 Unlucky influence (4)
13 Invent (8)
14 Armorial studies (8)
15 Funeral pile (4)
17 Fairness (6)
18 Narrate (6)
20 Eye shield (5)
22 Undergarment (3)

86

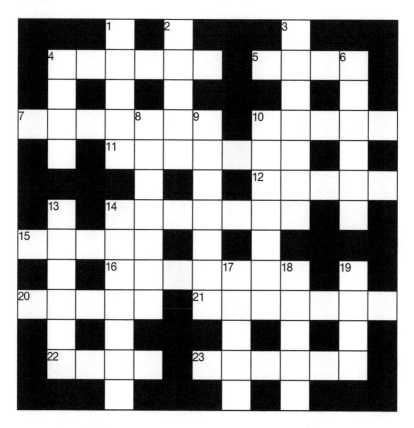

ACROSS

4 Grieg's Piano Concerto in —— (1,5)
5 Norfolk town (4)
7 Sikh head coverings (7)
10 T S —— (poet) (5)
11 Sketch, delineate (7)
12 English county (5)
14 Masters (anag.) (7)
15 Dissent (5)
16 Stokers (7)
20 Israeli orange (5)
21 Citizen Kane's last word (7)
22 Roman emperor (4)
23 CI; cow (6)

DOWN

1 West Indian dance (5)
2 —— Sinai (5)
3 Without purpose (7)
4 Aluminium/potassium sulphate (4)
6 Got a goal (6)
8 Strauss country (7)
9 Glossier (7)
10 Foes (7)
13 Stay (6)
14 Undergoes (7)
17 *Old Testament* lawgiver (5)
18 Full of gossip (5)
19 Anger (4)

ACROSS

1 Rank (6)
4 Part of shoe (5)
8 Contest (5)
9 Young swans (7)
10 Backache (7)
11 Thought (4)
12 Argument (3)
14 Italian volcano (4)
15 Graven image (4)
18 Cap (3)
21 Animal skin (4)
23 Moral (7)
25 Cause suffering to (7)
26 Blusher (5)
27 Planet; soil (5)
28 Proprietors (6)

DOWN

1 Elementary (6)
2 Try (7)
3 Turbulence (8)
4 Impulse (4)
5 Beg (5)
6 Scallywag (6)
7 Thespian (5)
13 Retreat (8)
16 Cut or shut off (7)
17 Put into words; a few words (6)
19 Liabilities (5)
20 Changes (6)
22 Delay (5)
24 Desire (4)

88

ACROSS

1 Snap (5)
4 From Helsinki? (7)
8 Move back; sanctuary (7)
9 Motet (anag.) (5)
10 Wear away (5)
11 Lassitude (7)
13 So be it (4)
15 Modernise (6)
17 Out-of-date (3,3)
20 *Compos mentis* (4)
22 John the —— (7)
24 Elk (5)
26 Garlic mayonnaise (5)
27 Adjective (7)
28 Committee-matters (7)
29 Avarice (5)

DOWN

1 Upstart (7)
2 Surpass (5)
3 Gorge (7)
4 In vain (6)
5 Unacceptable (3,2)
6 Honestly (2,5)
7 Greek poet (5)
12 Shortly (4)
14 Service dining-area (4)
16 Express disgust (7)
18 Northern rodent (7)
19 Given medical care (7)
21 Greek capital (6)
22 Well done! (5)
23 A work by 7 (5)
25 Brownish-yellow (5)

ACROSS

1 Sprite (5)
4 Dog; end (4)
8 Draw out (anag.) (7)
9 Youthful (5)
10 Recognised (5)
11 Preserving in brine (7)
13 —— Blethyn, actress (6)
15 Stint (6)
17 Fervent love (7)
20 Highways (5)
22 Buzz (5)
23 Gaining points (7)
24 Remain (4)
25 Underwater navigation device (5)

DOWN

1 Group of sheep (5)
2 Torn revision (anag.) (12)
3 Longed (7)
4 They ebb and flow (5)
5 Happy period (5)
6 Ritual cleansing (12)
7 Difference between generations (3,3)
12 Donkey (3)
13 Upright creatures (6)
14 Past (3)
16 Cardboard containers (7)
18 Passive (5)
19 Unpleasant (5)
21 —— Ray Robinson (5)

90

ACROSS

1 Overacts (colloq.) (4)
3 1970s PM; swing band leader (3,5)
9 —— Blackman (actress) (5)
10 Vacation (7)
11 Insane (3)
13 Sane place (anag.) (9)
14 Parade; egg; lily (6)
16 Stretch of time (6)
18 pm (9)
20 Not on (3)
22 In the direction of (7)
23 Day and —— (5)
25 Compasses with legs (8)
26 English spa city (4)

DOWN

1 Interjection (2-3)
2 Vassal; chess piece (3)
4 Resounds (6)
5 Papal court (4,3)
6 Slightly faster than walking pace (mus.) (9)
7 Had eyes (anag.) (7)
8 Jaunt (4)
12 Drying cloth (9)
14 Stretchy (7)
15 Pendant (7)
17 He uses a divining-rod (6)
19 Non-starter (colloq.) (2-2)
21 Go and get (5)
24 An Indian territory (3)

ACROSS

1 Tarnish (7)
8 —— Eisenhower (6)
9 Canvas shoe (7)
11 Recall (8)
12 Metrical feet (5)
14 Ashen (4)
15 The well-read (8)
17 Musical work (8)
18 Flat-topped hill (4)
20 Nobleman (5)
21 Enticing (8)
23 Divide into three (7)
24 Barrel-maker (6)
25 Unvarying (7)

DOWN

2 Nailer (anag.) (6)
3 Ill-tempered (6)
4 Eternally (4)
5 Add sugar (7)
6 Whisk (9)
7 Type of mountain grouse (9)
10 Receiver (9)
12 Not knowing (9)
13 Metal disc (9)
16 More husky (7)
18 French mountain range (6)
19 Football (6)
22 Ring (anag.) (4)

92

ACROSS

1 Numbers (7)
5 Trace (anag.) (5)
8 Rebuke (5)
9 Neck of land (7)
10 Tugging (7)
11 Adjust (5)
12 Appearance (6)
14 Save (6)
17 Licit (5)
19 Views; good wishes (7)
22 Scottish city (7)
23 Overhead (5)
24 Thick (5)
25 Rejoinder (7)

DOWN

1 Dubious (5)
2 Adult (5-2)
3 Spokes (5)
4 Miserly (6)
5 Small country house (7)
6 Lure (5)
7 Book; store (7)
12 Declared (7)
13 Refreshing scent (7)
15 Inquisitive (7)
16 Reward (anag.) (6)
18 Cereal (5)
20 Clutch (5)
21 Scandinavian; vegetable (5)

ACROSS

7 Supported (6)
8 Spookier (6)
10 Keep apart (7)
11 Heathen (5)
12 Strongly recommend (4)
13 Welcome (5)
17 Anxiety (5)
18 Mark of wound (4)
22 Scrub (5)
23 Explain and interpret (7)
24 Indifference (6)
25 Rue (6)

DOWN

1 Evident (7)
2 Skinflint (7)
3 Rot (5)
4 Puzzle (7)
5 Surface burn (5)
6 Vogue (5)
9 Pent up (9)
14 Lawlessness (7)
15 Accounts statistician (7)
16 Dryness (7)
19 Customary (5)
20 Muslim holy book (5)
21 Swiftness (5)

94

ACROSS

1 Refuse (6)
4 Mass meeting (5)
8 Walking-stick (5)
9 Large-billed bird (7)
10 Take in marriage (7)
11 Extravagant promotion (4)
12 Limb (3)
14 Spare (4)
15 Forearm bone (4)
18 Gratuity (3)
21 Japanese mount (4)
23 Antipathy (colloq.) (7)
25 Mixture for garden (7)
26 —— Borg, (tennis) (5)
27 Culinary herb (5)
28 Humbly (6)

DOWN

1 Attend (6)
2 Parties (anag.) (7)
3 Liquid waste (8)
4 Irritate (4)
5 Auspicious (5)
6 —— *Doodle*, song (6)
7 Salesman's patter (5)
13 Credulous (8)
16 Norwich's county (7)
17 Remnant (6)
19 eg Lasagne (5)
20 The capital of New South Wales (6)
22 Short crowbar (5)
24 Sole (4)

ACROSS

1 Love, worship (5)
4 *Messiah* composer (6)
9 Whole number (7)
10 Lotto (5)
11 Grecian vases (4)
12 Abdominal organs (7)
13 Beer (3)
14 Exposed; free (4)
16 Irish Gaelic (4)
18 Curious (3)
20 Scattered (7)
21 Competent (4)
24 Interior (5)
25 Slackened, relaxed (7)
26 Noised (anag.) (6)
27 Private teacher (5)

DOWN

1 Farewells (6)
2 Frequently (5)
3 Rim (4)
5 Waylaid (8)
6 Perils (7)
7 Washing aid (6)
8 Last resting place (5)
13 Sawn reed (anag.) (8)
15 Mum and Dad (7)
17 Inuit (6)
18 Smell (5)
19 Drinking jag (6)
22 Forthright (5)
23 Hit (4)

96

ACROSS

1 Received and understood (5)
4 Ground stone (4)
8 Mallets (7)
9 Beer mug (5)
10 Count —— (jazz) (5)
11 Examine (7)
13 "Of cloudless climes and —— skies" (Byron) (6)
15 Entrance (6)
17 Sin glut (anag.) (7)
20 Vistas (5)
22 Postponed (fig.) (2,3)
23 Lively, quick (mus.) (7)
24 Let it stand (L) (4)
25 Praise highly (5)

DOWN

1 Addicts' treatment (abbrev.) (5)
2 Art of scoring points (12)
3 Forest animal (3-4)
4 Japanese dish (5)
5 Beaks, conks (5)
6 Old gramophone record (7-5)
7 It's nil (anag.) (6)
12 Pinch; bite (3)
13 Fish, colour (6)
14 Longing (colloq.) (3)
16 —— & Wilbur Wright (7)
18 Clumsy (5)
19 Huge (5)
21 Mar (5)

ACROSS

1 European country (7)
5 Stun (4)
7 Relish (5)
8 Full of vapour (6)
10 Close imitation (4)
11 Shakespearean character (8)
13 Really (6)
14 Agency of the UN (6)
17 Lover of beauty (8)
19 Melon (4)
21 Former pupils (6)
22 Garlic 9 (5)
23 Liver's secretion (4)
24 9, 7 (7)

DOWN

1 Violently emotional (10)
2 Giggled (7)
3 Peak (4)
4 Reside (anag.) (6)
5 Putting clothes on (8)
6 Apathetic person (5)
9 7 for salad (10)
12 White 7 (8)
15 Italian woman (7)
16 Harsh (6)
18 Spicy 7 (5)
20 Young salmon (4)

98

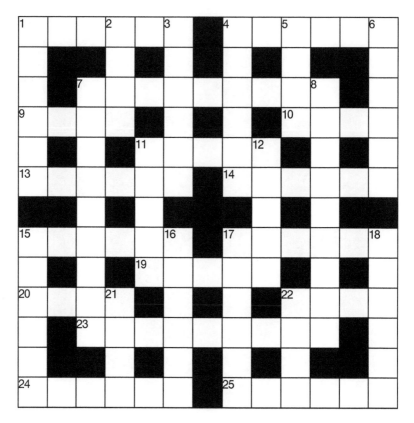

ACROSS

1 Supporter (6)
4 Gruff (6)
7 Many-legged insect (9)
9 Press; metal (4)
10 Slide (4)
11 Soak; precipitous (5)
13 Sofa (6)
14 Save (6)
15 Grease (anag.) (6)
17 Cut down manually (6)
19 Attain (5)
20 Brought forth (4)
22 Departed (4)
23 Administration (9)
24 Clatter (6)
25 Earthy (anag.) (6)

DOWN

1 Infants (6)
2 Ardent (4)
3 Go round (6)
4 Container, jumper (6)
5 Appends; Totals (4)
6 Please (anag.) (6)
7 Twisted (9)
8 Clear enunciation (9)
11 Lop off (5)
12 Luscious fruit (5)
15 Stroller (6)
16 Harsh, strict (6)
17 Whisky (6)
18 Vigour (6)
21 Restrict food-intake (4)
22 Spanish painter (4)

ACROSS

7 State firmly (6)
8 The BBC (coll.) (6)
10 Posture (7)
11 Mother-of-pearl (5)
12 Great merriment (4)
13 Leap (5)
17 Snap (5)
18 Corona (4)
22 Bitter (5)
23 Hold within (7)
24 Selected (6)
25 Collect (6)

DOWN

1 Rubbish (7)
2 Feeling remorse (7)
3 Follow (5)
4 Sly (7)
5 Soup base (5)
6 Revolt (5)
9 Lack of knowledge (9)
14 Grievances (7)
15 Elan (7)
16 Ironworks (7)
19 Contented (5)
20 Ploy (5)
21 Go furtively (5)

100

ACROSS

1 Going on foot (7)
5 Drives away (5)
8 Banter (5)
9 Soft sweet (7)
10 Enliven (7)
11 Twit (5)
12 Hose (6)
14 Bold-faced (6)
17 Bream (anag.) (5)
19 Grappling-iron (7)
22 Flourish (7)
23 Amid (5)
24 Humid; near (5)
25 Discourse (7)

DOWN

1 Witchcraft (5)
2 Tendency (7)
3 —— dig (5)
4 Boss (6)
5 Treason (anag.) (7)
6 Egg-shaped (5)
7 Attack (3,4)
12 Trade (7)
13 Row of houses (7)
15 American postal designation (3,4)
16 Skin complaint (6)
18 Game of chance (5)
20 Prize (5)
21 Ethiopian king (5)

ACROSS

1 Grasps (5)
4 Pierced (5)
10 Vegetable (7)
11 Urge forward (5)
12 Cherubs (5)
13 Keenly (7)
15 World's longest river (4)
17 Boasts (5)
19 Trove (anag.) (5)
22 Small road (4)
25 Deal in illicit drink (7)
27 Turns over (5)
29 Quotidian (5)
30 Scotland's flower (7)
31 Nimble (5)
32 Cable carrier (5)

DOWN

2 Moroccan city (5)
3 Compass point (7)
5 Due (5)
6 Ruler (7)
7 Range (5)
8 Gem (5)
9 Kills (5)
14 A vast age (4)
16 eg Skye (4)
18 Gin or It (anag.) (7)
20 Write poetry (7)
21 Home (5)
23 Decorative stone (5)
24 Deathly pale (5)
26 True (5)
28 Bingo (5)

102

ACROSS

1 Cook (4)
5 Goldie ——, actress (4)
7 Copy (7)
8 Small clothes shop (8)
10 Container for flowers (4)
12 —— Redding, singer (4)
14 Turkish city (8)
16 Ominous (8)
17 Ascetic discipline (4)
18 Joke (4)
19 Unmarried woman (8)
22 Keep out (7)
23 Overtake (4)
24 Wacky (4)

DOWN

1 Crustacean (4)
2 Decree (4)
3 Unease (8)
4 Secure (4)
5 Celestial (8)
6 Back of neck (4)
9 Summary (7)
11 Convey illegally (7)
13 Game in alley (8)
15 eg Paddington (8)
18 Leap (4)
19 Bag (4)
20 Port by canal (4)
21 Precious red stone (4)

ACROSS

1 Jetties (5)
5 Scene —— crime (2,3)
8 Empire (5)
9 Emile (anag.) (5)
10 Soviet city now St Petersburg (9)
11 Impudence (3)
12 Disrobe next (anag.) (11)
15 Confident of one's own ideas (4-7)
19 Deciduous tree (3)
20 Two cards of a suit (9)
22 Drive out (5)
23 William II's nickname (5)
24 Sinned (5)
25 eg Samoyed (5)

DOWN

1 Unequalled (8)
2 Immune (6)
3 Asian country (3,5)
4 Sandwich (informal) (6)
5 Sign (4)
6 Insect's upper body (6)
7 —— out: increased (4)
13 Titled lady (8)
14 Sentimentality (8)
16 More noisy (6)
17 Counterbalance (3,3)
18 Old Greek city (6)
20 —— Ellington (jazz musician) (4)
21 Peer (4)

104

ACROSS

4 Female sibling (6)
5 Cold-shoulder (4)
7 Arched (7)
10 Shocks (5)
11 Seafarer (7)
12 Striped animal (5)
14 Mass for the dead (7)
15 Arabian republic (5)
16 Became mature (7)
20 Female fox (5)
21 Please greatly (7)
22 Sound of owl (4)
23 Octave (anag.) (6)

DOWN

1 Palms (anag.) (5)
2 Ague (5)
3 Statement to be proved in maths (7)
4 Burglar's loot (4)
6 Disposition (6)
8 Deceived (5,2)
9 Watered down (7)
10 Wicked wife of Ahab (7)
13 Opposite of nadir (6)
14 Church screen (7)
17 Audacity (5)
18 Party with records (5)
19 Informal talk (4)

ANSWERS

1

Across
1 Wind
4 Cheetah
8 Delicacy
9 Rib
11 Anthem
13 Tenant
14 Litre
15 Kiev
17 Lest
18 Mitre
20 Ashram
21 Overdo
24 Mob
25 Vigilant
26 Nettled
27 Nine

Down
2 Inert
3 Drivel
4 Coax
5 Elysee
6 Tartare
7 Habitation
10 Backgammon
12 Minim
13 Truro
16 Exhibit
18 Marvel
19 Evelyn
22 Run in
23 Aged

2

Across
1 Close
4 Thais
10 Fetters
11 Noise
12 Event
13 Eustace
15 Ears
17 Share
19 Eager
22 Oust
25 Student
27 Titan
29 Aphis
30 Emitted
31 Gypsy
32 Asset

Down
2 Lithe
3 Spelter
5 Hands
6 Imitate
7 Often
8 Esher
9 Refer
14 Uses
16 Aeon
18 Haughty
20 Attains
21 Oscar
23 Utter
24 Snide
26 Eases
28 Title

3

Across
1 Delete
7 Hubbies
8 Veneered
9 Pulse
10 Nomad
11 Roar
12 Ideal
15 Babel
16 Yokel
19 Solo
20 Chant
21 React
22 Keepsake
23 Terrain
24 Greens

Down
1 Divinity
2 Landmark
3 Trend
4 Mud
5 Absurd
6 Geisha
7 Heartbroken
9 Pail
13 Escapade
14 Listless
15 Blot
17 Obeyed
18 Escort
20 Caper
22 Kid

4

Across

4 Ronald
5 Sway
7 Airport
10 Islay
11 Everest
12 Fault
14 Stellar
15 Hanoi
16 Douglas
20 Haydn
21 Yankees
22 Mann
23 Weevil

Down

1 Snipe
2 Blare
3 Two-star
4 Ruin
6 Yearly
8 Ovation
9 Trilogy
10 Isfahan
13 Napalm
14 Sodding
17 Lager
18 Skive
19 Peel

5

Across

1 Tracked
5 Table
8 Crest
9 Matured
10 Thigh-bone
12 Mar
13 Prompt
14 Apathy
17 Tea
18 Pentagram
20 Epicure
21 Sauna
23 Tinge
24 Tedious

Down

1 Tacit
2 Ape
3 Ketchup
4 Damson
5 Tithe
6 Barometer
7 Elderly
11 Isolation
13 Patient
15 Praised
16 Insect
18 Pause
19 Means
22 Ufo

6

Across

1 Foray
4 Nurse
10 Discard
11 Scour
12 Patio
13 Intense
15 Note
17 Vixen
19 Evade
22 Cede
25 Abdomen
27 Rival
29 Bacon
30 Reigned
31 Islam
32 Stems

Down

2 Onset
3 Abalone
5 Upset
6 Scorned
7 Adopt
8 Admit
9 Brief
14 Need
16 Once
18 Indicts
20 Verdict
21 Rabbi
23 Entry
24 Glade
26 Mania
28 Venom

7

Across
7 Parish
8 Shoots
10 Cascade
11 Truce
12 Flip
13 Agony
17 Kayak
18 Jeer
22 Drain
23 Cruelty
24 Oyster
25 Hector

Down
1 Specify
2 Prosaic
3 Usual
4 Whiting
5 Bogus
6 Asset
9 Vengeance
14 Launder
15 Zealots
16 Gruyere
19 Idiom
20 Marsh
21 Queen

8

Across
1 Robbing
5 Hood
7 Total
8 Avenge
10 Abet
11 Strainer
13 Tested
14 Accord
17 Negative
19 Stet
21 Sorrel
22 Amino
23 Amid
24 Neatens

Down
1 Retracting
2 Bothers
3 Ills
4 Giants
5 Hierarch
6 Organ
9 Traditions
12 Bettered
15 Outline
16 Avalon
18 Groom
20 Saga

9

Across
1 Toby
4 Perfect
8 Lyonesse
9 Tar
11 Amused
13 Vienna
14 Eerie
15 Kong
17 Mali
18 Viola
20 Unreal
21 Affirm
24 Two
25 Improved
26 East End
27 Doll

Down
2 Of you
3 Yankee
4 Pisa
5 Reekie
6 Estonia
7 Terra firma
10 Lacklustre
12 Devil
13 Villa
16 Nervous
18 Valise
19 Afford
22 Ideal
23 Sped

10

Across
1 Porto
4 Prance
9 Haiti
10 Capital
11 Nacelle
12 Sidon
14 & 15 Lie low
16 Imp
18 Air
21 Radar
22 Antenna
23 Relapse
25 Yucca
26 Tomato
27 Ninja

Down
1 Pahang
2 Rain-cloud
3 Oriole
5 Repose
6 Nut
7 Ealing
8 Accelerated
13 Dominican
17 Ararat
18 Armpit
19 Stay on
20 Canada
24 Lum

11

Across
1 Tails
4 Pinning
8 Tadpole
9 Maize
10 Exact
11 Codeine
13 Ewer
15 Serene
17 Angler
20 Able
22 Dislike
24 Guess
26 Raise
27 Theatre
28 Elector
29 Tenet

Down
1 Tatters
2 India
3 Shorten
4 Pierce
5 Nomad
6 Initial
7 Geese
12 Oral
14 Weak
16 Respite
18 Neglect
19 Respect
21 Better
22 Dirge
23 Inert
25 Eaten

12

Across
1 Forest
4 Heart
8 Depth
9 Labours
10 Nervous
11 Tell
12 Saw
14 Isle
15 Imam
18 Ram
21 Adds
23 Adheres
25 Accepts
26 Range
27 Mayor
28 Owners

Down
1 Fading
2 Reports
3 Schooner
4 Hobo
5 Azure
6 Tussle
7 Bless
13 Withdraw
16 Arrange
17 Napalm
19 Marsh
20 Assess
22 Decoy
24 Spur

13

Across
1 Coarse
7 Fishing
8 Sure-fire
9 Crook
10 Media
11 Norm
12 Asset
15 Sahib
16 Elect
19 Hate
20 Erato
21 Islay
22 Evensong
23 Welcome
24 Gideon

Down
1 Cashmere
2 Airedale
3 Sofia
4 Vie
5 Charms
6 Encore
7 French leave
9 Crab
13 Sycamore
14 Toboggan
15 Stay
17 Lesser
18 Chance
20 Ennui
22 Emu

14

Across
1 Fan
3 Sea
5 Full
7 Leads
8 Millet
10 Eden
11 Espouses
13 Totals
14 Veneto
17 Nembutal
19 Slav
21 Action
22 Coral
23 Ants
24 Par
25 Era

Down
1 Folkestone
2 Nearest
3 So-so
4 Almost
5 Fall over
6 Leeks
9 Aston Villa
12 Plaudits
15 Enlarge
16 Catnip
18 Macon
20 Scar

15

Across
1 Florenz
5 Night
8 Ingle
9 Scutari
10 Thistle
11 Indus
12 Angels
14 Throat
17 Nurse
19 Crimean
22 Reliant
23 Onset
24 El Cid
25 Hay Wain

Down
1 Flint
2 On-going
3 Event
4 Zester
5 Nourish
6 Grand
7 Twinset
12 Aintree
13 Leeward
15 Open sea
16 Scotch
18 Relic
20 Ivory
21 Not in

16

Across

1 Cross
4 Whirred
8 Puzzles
9 Ledge
10 Nisei
11 Entreat
13 Skye
15 St John
17 Agaric
20 Ogre
22 Peafowl
24 Nifty
26 Quick
27 Dormant
28 Erasmus
29 Lyric

Down

1 Copings
2 Oozes
3 Selfish
4 Wesley
5 Islet
6 Red deer
7 Dwelt
12 Near
14 Know
16 Juanita
18 General
19 Cryptic
21 Gladys
22 Pique
23 Oakum
25 Flair

17

Across

7 Billow
8 Stares
10 Notable
11 Twine
12 Over
13 Misty
17 Brave
18 Lake
22 Agent
23 Nothing
24 Resist
25 Plunge

Down

1 Abandon
2 Glitter
3 Doubt
4 Statute
5 Trait
6 Osier
9 Believing
14 Protest
15 Patient
16 Reigned
19 Hairy
20 Feast
21 Stalk

18

Across

1 Con
3 Few
5 Zion
7 Minor
8 Trader
10 Luke
11 Disorder
13 Muddle
14 Brecon
17 Numerous
19 Fuji
21 Exhort
22 Vetch
23 Upas
24 Ram
25 Red

Down

1 Compliment
2 Non-skid
3 Fork
4 Within
5 Zealotry
6 Oread
9 Brandished
12 Glorious
15 Clutter
16 Punter
18 Mix-up
20 Ovum

19

Across
1 Grilled
8 Stakes
9 Abjured
11 Dislodge
12 Stark
14 Were
15 Beheaded
17 Embolism
18 Plan
20 Alert
21 Cesspool
23 Nonagon
24 Routed
25 Revelry

Down
2 Rebate
3 Louvre
4 Eyed
5 Atelier
6 Skedaddle
7 Ascendant
10 Diversion
12 Sweetcorn
13 Arabesque
16 Clipper
18 Please
19 Arbour
22 Lone

20

Across
1 Palace
4 Aides
8 Oscar
9 Adamant
10 Erosion
11 User
12 Sip
14 Feng
15 Alga
18 Ere
21 Alps
23 Aridity
25 Apostle
26 Ninja
27 Among
28 Deedes

Down
1 Pro tem
2 Lactose
3 Carriage
4 Alas
5 Dials
6 Suture
7 Tarns
13 Patience
16 Grinned
17 Canada
19 Eager
20 Bylaws
22 Photo
24 Stag

21

Across
1 Bandeau
5 Leers
8 Sabot
9 Shatter
10 Corpulent
12 Rot
13 Raider
14 Attach
17 Sec
18 Tolerance
20 Leafage
21 Argue
23 Easel
24 Steeped

Down
1 Basic
2 Nab
3 Enthuse
4 Ulster
5 Least
6 Entertain
7 Stretch
11 Raincoats
13 Resolve
15 Terrace
16 Pliers
18 Trail
19 Emend
22 Gap

22

Across
1 Surgeon
5 Batch
8 He-man
9 Learner
10 Bullion
11 Agree
12 Abrupt
14 Strict
17 Eager
19 Loiters
22 Beached
23 Fling
24 Cupid
25 Earnest

Down
1 Sahib
2 Rambler
3 Ennui
4 Nylons
5 Blatant
6 Tenor
7 Harvest
12 Acerbic
13 Parched
15 Itemise
16 Pledge
18 Grasp
20 Infer
21 Sight

23

Across
1 Bridging
5 Lone
8 Caffeine
9 Fell
11 At all events
14 Ass
16 Inter
17 Aye
18 Measurement
21 Soda
22 Scribble
24 Nark
25 Stagnant

Down
1 Buck
2 Infra
3 Gregarious
4 Nun
6 Oceania
7 Enlisted
10 Overseeing
12 Lithe
13 Parmesan
15 Slander
19 Tibia
20 Beat
23 Cat

24

Across
1 Green
4 Peas
8 Entries
9 Aphid
10 Meath
11 Snooper
13 Fronds
15 Glared
17 Gradual
20 Rates
22 Opens
23 In haste
24 Stag
25 Sifts

Down
1 Gleam
2 Extrapolated
3 Neighed
4 Poses
5 Alamo
6 The Pirates of
7 Adored
12 Nag
13 Faggot
14 Spa
16 Larches
18 Upset
19 Lying
21 Steps

25

Across
1 Brie
5 Finn
7 Counter
8 Recorder
10 Evil
12 Lean
14 Retrieve
16 Mastered
17 Gasp
18 Veto
19 Progress
22 Andrews
23 Tall
24 Keen

Down
1 Beer
2 Echo
3 Murderer
4 Stir
5 Freezing
6 Noel
9 Everage
11 Invests
13 National
15 Tadpoles
18 Vast
19 Pads
20 Risk
21 Sean

26

Across
7 Alecks
8 Sander
10 Grahame
11 Belle
12 Tell
13 Phone
17 Giddy
18 Call
22 Magog
23 Strange
24 Litany
25 Blower

Down
1 Naughty
2 Default
3 Skean
4 Bambino
5 Oddly
6 Greet
9 Methodist
14 Ringing
15 Barn owl
16 Algebra
19 Imply
20 Agate
21 Grill

27

Across
1 Thyme
4 Untied
9 Martial
10 Gloom
11 Else
12 Cottage
13 Yak
14 Rove
16 Aped
18 Lap
20 Endorse
21 Ache
24 Capri
25 Germane
26 Ensign
27 Pilot

Down
1 Timber
2 Yarns
3 Exit
5 Nightcap
6 Isolate
7 Dampen
8 Pluck
13 Yearling
15 Oedipus
17 Rescue
18 Ledge
19 Select
22 Crawl
23 Grip

28

Across
1 Some
4 Assault
8 Infringe
9 Dam
11 Barrel
13 Overdo
14 Dunce
15 Lurk
17 Yogi
18 Minus
20 Indeed
21 Rattle
24 Nil
25 Barbaric
26 Eagerly
27 Echo

Down
2 Owner
3 Earned
4 Acne
5 Shelve
6 Undergo
7 Temporised
10 Ebullience
12 Lucid
13 Occur
16 Red flag
18 Member
19 Savage
22 Thigh
23 Dray

29

Across
1 Pair
4 Shaped
7 Eat
9 Knot
10 Agitated
11 Irk
12 Thin
13 Epidemic
16 Steeplechaser
19 Navigate
23 Roar
24 Moo
25 Balsamic
26 Skin
27 Ego
28 Nestle
29 Lank

Down
2 Anne Hathaway
3 Retinue
4 Stake
5 Alibi
6 Evade
8 Deliberation
14 Pleat
15 Doh
17 Pig
18 Aerosol
20 Issue
21 Admit
22 Emcee

30

Across
1 Runner
7 De Mille
8 Diameter
9 Sigma
10 Crest
11 Thin
12 Licit
15 Carat
16 Enter
19 Rain
20 Soave
21 Cream
22 Amethyst
23 Majesty
24 Boston

Down
1 Ridicule
2 Near East
3 Erect
4 Per
5 Rimini
6 Alumni
7 Deuteronomy
9 Silt
13 Catalyst
14 Tiverton
15 Cram
17 Norway
18 Erased
20 Set-to
22 Ate

31

Across
1 Ghana
4 Wash
8 That Man
9 Right
10 Outer
11 Mynheer
13 Albert
15 Morass
17 Zillion
20 Bring
22 Cutie
23 Darling
24 Stay
25 Egypt

Down
1 Get to
2 Adaptability
3 Admirer
4 Win 'em
5 Serin
6 Agreeability
7 Starts
12 Yam
13 Anzacs
14 Two
16 Osborne
18 Inept
19 Noddy
21 Gigot

32

Across
1 Mer
3 Say
5 Dees
7 Swing
8 Hearse
10 Orca
11 Sensilla
13 Darius
14 Secret
17 Castaway
19 Smee
21 Adroit
22 Rover
23 Knit
24 Bus
25 Lap

Down
1 Misconduct
2 Railcar
3 Sage
4 Yahweh
5 Dragster
6 Easel
9 Rattletrap
12 Runabout
15 Removal
16 Cantab
18 Sedan
20 Eros

33

Across
1 Mustered
7 Cedes
8 Distemper
9 Pen
10 Leek
11 Prompt
13 Rotten
14 Potage
17 Better
18 Pass
20 Tie
22 Insurgent
23 Reign
24 Snowdrop

Down
1 Model
2 Suspect
3 Even
4 Expire
5 Adept
6 Asinine
7 Crimson
12 Certain
13 Rapture
15 Amateur
16 Season
17 Begin
19 Set-up
21 Draw

34

Across

1 Struck
4 Share
8 Vague
9 Lecture
10 Getting
11 Feat
12 Sap
14 Daft
15 Arch
18 Saw
21 Back
23 Agitate
25 Advance
26 Nomad
27 Earns
28 Tender

Down

1 Savage
2 Regatta
3 Chemists
4 Sack
5 Acute
6 Ejects
7 Flags
13 Patience
16 Claimed
17 Ablaze
19 Wager
20 Gender
22 Cover
24 Onus

35

Across

4 Whinny
5 Fred
7 Disable
10 Salvo
11 Related
12 Glade
14 Pen name
15 Brief
16 Ginseng
20 Float
21 Tetanus
22 Coup
23 Finnan

Down

1 Bihar
2 Knell
3 Treadle
4 Weir
6 Divide
8 Benefit
9 Earnest
10 Segment
13 Frolic
14 Pegasus
17 Eerie
18 Gaunt
19 Ruin

36

Across

1 Winding
5 Rowed
8 Tidal
9 Measure
10 Headcloth
12 Dis
13 Laputa
14 Valour
17 Nor
18 Abandoned
20 Blatant
21 Rouge
23 Woden
24 Contend

Down

1 Watch
2 Nod
3 Illicit
4 Gambol
5 Reach
6 Wound down
7 Dresser
11 Ampersand
13 Longbow
15 Andiron
16 Baltic
18 Again
19 Dread
22 Ure

37

Across

1 Only
4 Foals
8 Endorses
9 Cert
10 Bias
11 Insisted
12 Verona
14 Rudder
16 Montague
19 Dell
20 Stab
21 Cribbage
22 Cargo
23 Hate

Down

2 Nooks
3 Yeshiva
4 Fasts
5 Accused
6 Spree
7 Engine
13 October
14 Rhenish
15 Eulogy
17 Optic
18 Gecko
19 Debut

38

Across

1 Trans
5 Sport
8 Asian
9 Troll
10 Erstwhile
11 Lei
12 Commonsense
15 Disengaging
19 Ear
20 Bubble-gum
22 Essen
23 Spain
24 Tryst
25 Three

Down

1 Totalled
2 Atomic
3 Salesman
4 Fiasco
5 Snow
6 Option
7 Type
13 Shipment
14 Entrance
16 Subway
17 Afghan
18 Geyser
20 Blot
21 List

39

Across

1 Prose
4 Cession
8 Element
9 Ensue
10 Eaten
11 Ecstasy
13 Alto
15 Tickle
17 Prates
20 Flee
22 Replete
24 Vista
26 Friar
27 Torrent
28 Erector
29 Enemy

Down

1 Pretext
2 Overt
3 Eternal
4 Cutlet
5 Seems
6 Instant
7 Needy
12 Cope
14 Left
16 Capsize
18 Reverie
19 Swarthy
21 Letter
22 Rifle
23 Egret
25 Swede

40

Across
1 Force
4 Aching
9 Canteen
10 Sepia
11 Lewd
12 Admired
13 Irk
14 Till
16 Rule
18 Ape
20 Adjourn
21 Lamb
24 Corgi
25 Obliges
26 Rodent
27 Shred

Down
1 Facile
2 Renew
3 Epée
5 Cashmere
6 Imperil
7 Guards
8 Sneak
13 Illusion
15 Injured
17 Dancer
18 Annoy
19 Abased
22 Augur
23 Alas

41

Across
1 Booker
4 Wrest
8 Haste
9 Twinges
10 Naughty
11 Free
12 Spa
14 Keen
15 Dull
18 Tow
21 Idea
23 Require
25 Passion
26 Azure
27 Rhyme
28 Delete

Down
1 Behind
2 Obscure
3 Elephant
4 Whim
5 Eager
6 Tested
7 Stays
13 Adequate
16 Leisure
17 Kipper
19 Wrong
20 Severe
22 Essay
24 Vice

42

Across
1 Quay
4 Bored
8 Tribunal
9 Grog
10 Spur
11 Trammels
12 Baffle
14 Denial
16 Bungalow
19 Kite
20 Dart
21 Baguette
22 Errol
23 Rada

Down
2 Umber
3 Yangtze
4 Balsa
5 Regimen
6 Droll
7 Grappa
13 Fighter
14 Dowager
15 Astute
17 Usage
18 Label
19 Knead

43

Across

1 Monarch
8 Offaly
9 Surveys
11 Speak out
12 Carry
14 Erat
15 Sturgeon
17 Transfer
18 Here
20 Carer
21 Imitates
23 Dangers
24 Louder
25 Depends

Down

2 Ocular
3 Advert
4 Cays
5 Affairs
6 Barometer
7 Bystander
10 Spattered
12 Certainly
13 Rapacious
16 Escaped
18 Haggle
19 Reared
22 Sage

44

Across

1 Wore
5 Sing
7 Matilda
8 Coolibar
10 Tabu
12 Mate
14 Infra dig
16 Tintagel
17 Eden
18 Anna
19 Test case
22 Cabinet
23 Ogre
24 Yomp

Down

1 WRAC
2 Emil
3 Stabling
4 Slur
5 Salt Lake
6 Guru
9 Oration
11 Baileys
13 Entrance
15 Folk song
18 Arno
19 Toby
20 City
21 Earp

45

Across

1 Racquets
5 Port
8 Creation
9 Stoa
11 Shuttlecock
14 Cur
16 Helot
17 Ego
18 Adjournment
21 Boil
22 Zimbabwe
24 Even
25 Dead-heat

Down

1 Ruck
2 Chess
3 Untruthful
4 Two
6 Outcome
7 Thank you
10 Featherbed
12 Talon
13 Scrabble
15 Rejoice
19 Table
20 Text
23 Ire

46

Across
1 Pique
4 Hocks
10 Precise
11 Eclat
12 Igloo
13 Elation
15 Rode
17 Thing
19 Adage
22 Rare
25 Manager
27 Allow
29 Staff
30 Overdue
31 Adder
32 Lying

Down
2 Ideal
3 Unicorn
5 Omega
6 Killing
7 Spoil
8 Vexed
9 Stunt
14 Lear
16 Ogre
18 Hansard
20 Deanery
21 Amass
23 Arrow
24 Owner
26 Gaffe
28 Laden

47

Across
4 Offers
5 Tyke
7 Cheer up
10 Enter
11 Retrace
12 State
14 Permits
15 Belle
16 Impulse
20 Alias
21 Maypole
22 Male
23 Gaucho

Down
1 After
2 Trout
3 Cygnets
4 Oche
6 Erects
8 Redeems
9 Premium
10 Ecstasy
13 Bedlam
14 Pliable
17 La Paz
18 Epoch
19 Also

48

Across
1 Surplice
7 Stock
8 Masterful
9 Apt
10 Eddy
11 Carver
13 Gaelic
14 Brawny
17 Spigot
18 Grip
20 Yet
22 Lubricant
23 Raise
24 Stealthy

Down
1 Somme
2 Residue
3 Leer
4 Caftan
5 Solar
6 Sketchy
7 Slavery
12 Risible
13 Gruyère
15 Warrant
16 Combat
17 Stain
19 Pithy
21 Riga

49

Across

1 Herein
4 Their
8 Aspic
9 Russian
10 Ensured
11 Nero
12 Ebb
14 Sere
15 Oust
18 Dis
21 Glib
23 Candour
25 America
26 Extra
27 Title
28 Asides

Down

1 Heaven
2 Riposte
3 Incurred
4 Task
5 Exile
6 Random
7 Erode
13 Bouncers
16 Spotted
17 Aghast
19 Scrap
20 Breaks
22 Inert
24 Pile

50

Across

1 One
3 Sup
5 Honor
8 Thyme
9 Puppies
10 Crib
11 Treeless
13 Camber
14 Hearts
17 Diamonds
19 Smew
22 Lessens
23 Story
24 Soppy
25 Nye
26 Eon

Down

1 Optic
2 Elysium
3 Suez
4 Papers
5 Happened
6 Noise
7 Resists
12 Recovery
13 Cuddles
15 Rumpole
16 Edison
18 Aesop
20 Way in
21 Isle

51

Across

1 Door
4 Chester
8 Weymouth
9 Mum
11 Rhesus
13 Peseta
14 Stood
15 & 17 Portland
18 Jelly
20 Signed
21 Easter
24 Eft
25 Bridport
26 Swanage
27 Dank

Down

2 Obese
3 Rumpus
4 Clue
5 Echoed
6 Tempera
7 Ram-raiders
10 Prepossess
12 Steed
13 Poole
16 Regatta
18 Jerboa
19 Yapped
22 Turin
23 Wine

52

Across

7 Wirral

8 Havana

9 Summer holiday

10 Stone Age

12 Acts

13 Ibid

15 Listless

17 Monday morning

19 Plucky

20 Answer

Down

1 Minuet

2 Promenade-deck

3 Slur

4 Shooters

5 Availableness

6 Intact

11 All my eye

14 Brolly

16 Sunset

18 Oban

53

Across

4 Chores

5 Push

7 Admired

10 Relax

11 Deliver

12 Maker

14 General

15 Ruler

16 Seasons

20 Write

21 Eastern

22 Warn

23 Vision

Down

1 Solid

2 Jewel

3 Funeral

4 Code

6 Heaven

8 Referee

9 Disease

10 Remains

13 Burrow

14 Gesture

17 Oasis

18 Strip

19 Iron

54

Across

1 Honour

4 Count

8 Ascot

9 Tension

10 Steamer

11 Sell

12 Top

14 Writ

15 Roam

18 Ewe

21 Aide

23 Aspires

25 Refusal

26 Rinse

27 Dares

28 Oddest

Down

1 Hoarse

2 Nuclear

3 Ultimate

4 Cane

5 Unite

6 Tangle

7 Start

13 Prepared

16 Arrange

17 Sacred

19 Eagle

20 Assent

22 Defer

24 Asks

55

Across
1 Deadly
4 Tocsin
7 Analgesic
9 Hide
10 Cant
11 Colic
13 Meadow
14 Sapper
15 Resume
17 Sonnet
19 Atone
20 Flak
22 Alga
23 Mainframe
24 Mystic
25 Drowse

Down
1 Durham
2 Done
3 Yellow
4 Thesis
5 Chic
6 Natter
7 Ad nauseam
8 Campanile
11 Comma
12 Canoe
15 Reform
16 Ethnic
17 Snared
18 Trance
21 Kant
22 Ammo

56

Across
1 Foreign
5 Daft
7 Untie
8 Report
10 Dank
11 Macaroni
13 Tremor
14 Censor
17 Obstacle
19 Mess
21 Entice
22 Lapse
23 Jest
24 Torrent

Down
1 Foundation
2 Retinue
3 Idea
4 Normal
5 Depraved
6 Forgo
9 Disrespect
12 Vocalist
15 Steeple
16 Client
18 Singe
20 Slur

57

Across
1 Hallways
7 Taper
8 Telephone
9 Col
10 Hear
11 Legacy
13 Mayday
14 Plenty
17 Mazuma
18 Dosh
20 Era
22 Role model
23 Euros
24 Steady on

Down
1 Hatch
2 Lullaby
3 Wipe
4 Yeomen
5 Spicy
6 Trolley
7 Tenable
12 Panzers
13 Moneyed
15 Noonday
16 Amulet
17 Marry
19 Helen
21 Emma

58

Across
1 Go in
4 Wither
7 Ego
9 Levi
10 Rotation
11 Tot
12 Wish
13 Hilarity
16 Recrimination
19 Entreaty
23 Curb
24 Irk
25 Osculate
26 Lied
27 Lee
28 Shrewd
29 Deft

Down
2 One-sidedness
3 Neither
4 Worth
5 Total
6 Eater
8 Do-it-yourself
14 Idiot
15 Aga
17 Ice
18 Tackled
20 Rough
21 Amaze
22 Yield

59

Across
1 Colour
4 Untie
8 Rinse
9 Oversee
10 Sheared
11 Type
12 All
14 Itch
15 Urge
18 Sap
21 Chat
23 Recluse
25 Elastic
26 Ember
27 Misty
28 Intend

Down
1 Cerise
2 Lenient
3 Unearths
4 Used
5 Testy
6 Eleven
7 Gouda
13 Luncheon
16 Grumble
17 Scream
19 Price
20 Neared
22 Amass
24 Stay

60

Across
1 Ode
3 Ear
5 Watt
7 Candy
8 Matter
10 Bebe
11 Intrepid
13 Treaty
14 Inform
17 Estimate
19 Lean
21 Object
22 Amaze
23 Kyle
24 Spa
25 Lie

Down
1 Once bitten
2 Ennoble
3 Etym
4 Romany
5 Watering
6 Tie up
9 Adam and Eve
12 Stampede
15 Overall
16 Status
18 Tubby
20 Java

61

Across
1 Doh
3 See
5 Dough
8 Slide
9 Beguine
10 Obey
11 Flamenco
13 Dosi-do
14 Deafen
17 Approval
19 Axed
22 Gavotte
23 Aaron
24 Tinny
25 Ail
26 Toe

Down
1 Disco
2 Heiress
3 Step
4 Embalm
5 Degummed
6 Union
7 Hoedown
12 Adroitly
13 Draught
15 Foxtrot
16 Valeta
18 Pavan
20 Dance
21 Ball

62

Across
7 Injure
8 Notion
10 Package
11 Alarm
12 Anew
13 Spook
17 Hoard
18 Wept
22 Clear
23 Dormant
24 Onager
25 Repair

Down
1 Display
2 Ejected
3 Break
4 Donator
5 Vital
6 Enemy
9 Desperado
14 Gourmet
15 Getaway
16 Stature
19 Actor
20 Legal
21 Order

63

Across
1 Weigh
4 Twine
10 Purpose
11 Gaudi
12 Ashen
13 Control
15 Deep
17 Balsa
19 Early
22 Sand
25 Adapted
27 Virus
29 Index
30 Ignoble
31 Inane
32 Cease

Down
2 Earth
3 Grounds
5 Wagon
6 Neutral
7 Appal
8 Fence
9 Fills
14 Open
16 Ease
18 Abandon
20 Advance
21 Cabin
23 Admit
24 Asked
26 Toxin
28 Robes

64

Across
1 Lei
3 Preacher
9 Renal
10 Petrify
11 Air
13 Dismissal
14 Orchid
16 Verity
18 Fruitless
20 Tub
22 Cringer
23 Cabot
25 Rye grass
26 Ely

Down
1 Larva
2 Inn
4 Repast
5 Astaire
6 Hair shirt
7 Royalty
8 Plod
12 Reclusive
14 Officer
15 Integer
17 Debris
19 Sack
21 Batty
24 Bye

65

Across
1 Are
3 Gar
5 Saga
7 Theme
8 Muppet
10 Glad
11 Estrange
13 Totals
14 Stifle
17 Emeritus
19 Brat
21 Cantab
22 Bambi
23 Tear
24 Bee
25 Nun

Down
1 Altogether
2 Elegant
3 Glen
4 Remiss
5 Separate
6 Green
9 Pedestrian
12 Cloister
15 Fireman
16 Hubbub
18 Evade
20 Able

66

Across
1 Dee
3 Mag
5 Niffy
8 Scent
9 Savarin
10 Yang
11 Language
13 Bullet
14 Stamps
17 Young man
19 Aqua
22 Nutters
23 Ideal
24 Run in
25 Mum
26 New

Down
1 Dishy
2 Eternal
3 Mute
4 Gustav
5 Navigate
6 Forma
7 Yonkers
12 Sea-green
13 Brynner
15 McQueen
16 Ransom
18 Upton
20 Allow
21 Film

67

Across
1 Ayr
3 Apparent
9 Layer
10 A priori
11 Aft
13 Prestwick
14 Girvan
16 Advise
18 Tobermory
20 Met
22 Israeli
23 Rodeo
25 Keystone
26 Gin

Down
1 Alloa
2 Ray
4 Planet
5 Aerated
6 Eroticism
7 Trickle
8 Crop
12 Turnberry
14 Gatwick
15 Airiest
17 Lotion
19 York
21 Troon
24 Dig

68

Across
7 Cruise
8 Sibyls
10 Radiant
11 Taste
12 Tiny
13 Broke
17 Title
18 Pull
22 Tread
23 Stature
24 Violin
25 Mature

Down
1 Accrete
2 Pudding
3 Essay
4 Mistake
5 Gypsy
6 Asked
9 Sterilise
14 Disdain
15 Tumulus
16 Altered
19 Stove
20 Below
21 Canal

69

Across
1 Rake
4 Jorvik
7 Moo
9 Chop
10 Lay waste
11 Rot
12 Cede
13 Soldered
16 New South Wales
19 Serenade
23 Ruse
24 Rap
25 Stranger
26 Onus
27 Oar
28 Pester
29 Toga

Down
2 Achievements
3 Empress
4 Jolts
5 Royal
6 Irate
8 St Petersburg
14 Opted
15 Dew
17 Own
18 Airport
20 Erase
21 Angst
22 Error

70

Across
1 Fugit
5 Tiffs
8 Earth
9 Lover
10 Traveller
11 Own
12 Grasshopper
15 Happy medium
19 Axe
20 Advocates
22 Incus
23 Gecko
24 Beefy
25 Natal

Down
1 Falmouth
2 Giving
3 Tertiary
4 Trials
5 Thee
6 Fillip
7 Seer
13 Omission
14 Reversal
16 Pavane
17 Entice
18 Mascot
20 Ahab
21 Cagy

71

Across
1 Scent
4 Turf
7 Hold
8 Yeomanry
9 Bronze Age
10 & 16 All but
12 Invert
14 Thrown
16 See 10
18 Jerusalem
21 Quixotic
22 Heel
23 Lyre
24 Erred

Down
1 Sporran
2 Endanger
3 Thyme
4 Teak
5 Rural
6 Fought
11 Breather
13 Treaty
15 Weekend
17 Usury
19 Uncle
20 Axle

72

Across
1 Jubilee
5 Fall
7 Youre
8 Tolled
10 Arum
11 Marooned
13 Kitten
14 Kennel
17 Radiator
19 Twee
21 Window
22 Aroma
23 Skid
24 Beastie

Down
1 Jaywalkers
2 Bouquet
3 Leek
4 Extras
5 Fell over
6 Lie in
9 Adulterate
12 Regarded
15 Newport
16 Cobweb
18 Drink
20 Ta-ta

73

Across
1 Buzz
5 Bees
7 Examine
8 Obstacle
10 Ashy
12 Prod
14 Machismo
16 Strainer
17 Grub
18 Fawn
19 Pilotage
22 Stetson
23 Kite
24 Aqua

Down
1 Brio
2 Zest
3 Fancy man
4 Jive
5 Behaving
6 Sway
9 Biretta
11 Homburg
13 Diagnose
15 Careless
18 Flak
19 Pier
20 Tuna
21 Elba

74

Across
1 Queue
4 Weight
9 Avarice
10 Guile
11 Ewes
12 Regular
13 Try
14 Aria
16 Nude
18 Dog
20 Reserve
21 Mail
24 Cling
25 Swifter
26 Skinny
27 Egret

Down
1 Quaver
2 Erase
3 Evil
5 Engaging
6 Grilled
7 Theory
8 Weary
13 Tarragon
15 Rossini
17 Cracks
18 Dense
19 Claret
22 Actor
23 Dire

75

Across
1 Thumb
4 Asses
10 Licence
11 Light
12 Upset
13 Clement
15 Echo
17 Sheer
19 Study
22 Oath
25 Triceps
27 Ratio
29 Motor
30 Elation
31 Adore
32 Aside

Down
2 Hacks
3 Manatee
5 Solve
6 Egghead
7 Flout
8 Teach
9 State
14 Lost
16 Crop
18 Hoisted
20 Threats
21 Stump
23 Asked
24 Mound
26 Error
28 Tried

76

Across

1 Wrest
4 Full
7 Ring
8 Terminus
9 Asininity
10 Dye
12 Unwell
14 Lively
16 Ivy
18 Substance
21 Endanger
22 Rift
23 Pest
24 Boxer

Down

1 Whitsun
2 Engender
3 Titan
4 Fail
5 Lousy
6 Brutal
11 Aviatrix
13 Lounge
15 Lucifer
17 Venue
19 Scrub
20 Cast

77

Across

1 Warts
4 Sarong
9 Lambast
10 Cater
11 Eats
12 Evident
13 Row
14 Mate
16 Elsa
18 ATS
20 Distend
21 Toga
24 Larne
25 Prevent
26 Donate
27 Paste

Down

1 Wallet
2 Remit
3 Sham
5 Archives
6 Outlets
7 Gyrate
8 Strew
13 Reverent
15 Also-ran
17 Addled
18 Adept
19 Cattle
22 Omens
23 Keep

78

Across

1 Iambic
7 Humming
8 Enslaved
9 Bayou
10 Eerie
11 Dear
12 Stash
15 Brash
16 Sisal
19 Soft
20 Bound
21 Fight
22 Prospero
23 Pleases
24 Blithe

Down

1 Icebergs
2 Mistress
3 Irate
4 Dud
5 Impart
6 Snoops
7 Headmasters
9 Bash
13 Argument
14 Handsome
15 Blot
17 Icicle
18 Ashlar
20 Basil
22 Pen

79

Across

4 Parley
5 View
7 Anglais
10 Genre
11 Lump sum
12 Ample
14 Signora
15 Crumb
16 Oldster
20 Unite
21 Hedonic
22 Heel
23 German

Down

1 Grill
2 Denim
3 Dilemma
4 Pony
6 Warble
8 Audible
9 Spanish
10 Guarded
13 French
14 Smother
17 Tenet
18 Roomy
19 Lion

80

Across

1 Maugham
5 Monet
8 Riper
9 Discern
10 Eternal
11 Aisle
12 Finish
14 Vacant
17 Agree
19 Elegant
22 Chablis
23 Again
24 Ditch
25 Spectre

Down

1 Merge
2 Umpteen
3 Heron
4 Middle
5 Mascara
6 Needs
7 Tangent
12 Flaccid
13 Stealth
15 Adamant
16 Census
18 Roast
20 Erase
21 Tonne

81

Across

7 Weight
8 Saturn
10 Anguish
11 Crete
12 Eros
13 Bogus
17 Maori
18 Stye
22 Perth
23 Camelot
24 Callas
25 Renoir

Down

1 Sweater
2 Kingdom
3 Chair
4 Bacchus
5 Rupee
6 Andes
9 Theocracy
14 Baghdad
15 Stilton
16 Reuters
19 Space
20 Troll
21 Amber

82

Across
1 Silly
4 Aisles
9 Halfwit
10 Degas
11 Onyx
12 Macrame
13 Rip
14 Fade
16 Nude
18 Tat
20 Hauteur
21 Feta
24 Drill
25 Scapula
26 Deemed
27 Biped

Down
1 School
2 Lolly
3 Yawn
5 Indecent
6 Laggard
7 Sister
8 Stump
13 Reveille
15 Abusive
17 Chided
18 Tryst
19 Hazard
22 Equip
23 Barb

83

Across
1 Booked
4 Oaken
8 Grief
9 Laggard
10 Torquay
11 Fell
12 Saw
14 Anti
15 Hump
18 Ass
21 Type
23 Cezanne
25 Lexicon
26 Keats
27 Green
28 Advent

Down
1 Bogota
2 Omicron
3 Effluvia
4 Orgy
5 Knave
6 Nodule
7 Plays
13 Whizz-kid
16 Mandate
17 Stalag
19 Scone
20 Jet set
22 Pixie
24 Scan

84

Across
7 Brides
8 Eddery
10 Visited
11 Mango
12 Used
13 Scoop
17 Rusts
18 Neon
22 Asdic
23 Outcome
24 Greasy
25 & 19 Evelyn Waugh

Down
1 Above us
2 Minster
3 Heath
4 Adamson
5 Jenny
6 Byron
9 Education
14 Success
15 Remould
16 Inferno
19 See 25
20 Idler
21 Steve

85

Across
- **1** Wicker
- **7** Swirled
- **8** Remedial
- **9** Jacob
- **10** Wooer
- **11** Vain
- **12** Neigh
- **15** Phlox
- **16** Ferry
- **19** Erst
- **20** Viola
- **21** Guile
- **22** Blizzard
- **23** Stature
- **24** Artery

Down
- **1** Werewolf
- **2** Commoner
- **3** Eider
- **4** Awl
- **5** Arcane
- **6** Belong
- **7** Sal volatile
- **9** Jinx
- **13** Innovate
- **14** Heraldry
- **15** Pyre
- **17** Equity
- **18** Relate
- **20** Vizor
- **22** Bra

86

Across
- **4** A minor
- **5** Diss
- **7** Turbans
- **10** Eliot
- **11** Outline
- **12** Essex
- **14** Streams
- **15** Demur
- **16** Firemen
- **20** Jaffa
- **21** Rosebud
- **22** Nero
- **23** Jersey

Down
- **1** Limbo
- **2** Mount
- **3** Aimless
- **4** Alum
- **6** Scored
- **8** Austria
- **9** Sleeker
- **10** Enemies
- **13** Remain
- **14** Suffers
- **17** Moses
- **18** Newsy
- **19** Fury

87

Across
- **1** Status
- **4** Upper
- **8** Match
- **9** Cygnets
- **10** Lumbago
- **11** Idea
- **12** Row
- **14** Etna
- **15** Idol
- **18** Lid
- **21** Hide
- **23** Ethical
- **25** Afflict
- **26** Rouge
- **27** Earth
- **28** Owners

Down
- **1** Simple
- **2** Attempt
- **3** Upheaval
- **4** Urge
- **5** Plead
- **6** Rascal
- **7** Actor
- **13** Withdraw
- **16** Occlude
- **17** Phrase
- **19** Debts
- **20** Alters
- **22** Defer
- **24** Wish

88

Across
1 Photo
4 Finnish
8 Retreat
9 Totem
10 Erode
11 Languor
13 Amen
15 Update
17 Old hat
20 Sane
22 Baptist
24 Moose
26 Aioli
27 Epithet
28 Agendas
29 Greed

Down
1 Parvenu
2 Outdo
3 Overeat
4 Futile
5 Not on
6 In truth
7 Homer
12 Anon
14 Mess
16 Deplore
18 Lemming
19 Treated
21 Athens
22 Brava
23 Iliad
25 Ochre

89

Across
1 Fairy
4 Tail
8 Outward
9 Young
10 Known
11 Salting
13 Brenda
15 Scrimp
17 Passion
20 Roads
22 Drone
23 Scoring
24 Stay
25 Sonar

Down
1 Flock
2 Introversion
3 Yearned
4 Tides
5 Idyll
6 Purification
7 Age gap
12 Ass
13 Bipeds
14 Ago
16 Cartons
18 Inert
19 Nasty
21 Sugar

90

Across
1 Hams
3 Ted Heath
9 Honor
10 Holiday
11 Mad
13 Pleasance
14 Easter
16 Period
18 Afternoon
20 Off
22 Towards
23 Night
25 Calipers
26 Bath

Down
1 Ho-hum
2 Man
4 Echoes
5 Holy See
6 Andantino
7 Hayseed
8 Trip
12 Dishtowel
14 Elastic
15 Eardrop
17 Dowser
19 No-no
21 Fetch
24 Goa

91

Across

1 Blacken
8 Dwight
9 Sneaker
11 Remember
12 Iambi
14 Grey
15 Literati
17 Oratorio
18 Mesa
20 Baron
21 Alluring
23 Trisect
24 Cooper
25 Uniform

Down

2 Linear
3 Crabby
4 Ever
5 Sweeten
6 Eggbeater
7 Ptarmigan
10 Recipient
12 Ignorance
13 Medallion
16 Hoarser
18 Massif
19 Soccer
22 Grin

92

Across

1 Figures
5 Cater
8 Scold
9 Isthmus
10 Yanking
11 Alter
12 Aspect
14 Rescue
17 Legal
19 Regards
22 Glasgow
23 Above
24 Dense
25 Riposte

Down

1 Fishy
2 Grown-up
3 Radii
4 Stingy
5 Cottage
6 Tempt
7 Reserve
12 Alleged
13 Cologne
15 Curious
16 Drawer
18 Grain
20 Grasp
21 Swede

93

Across

7 Backed
8 Eerier
10 Isolate
11 Pagan
12 Urge
13 Greet
17 Angst
18 Scar
22 Scour
23 Expound
24 Apathy
25 Regret

Down

1 Obvious
2 Scrooge
3 Decay
4 Perplex
5 Singe
6 Trend
9 Repressed
14 Anarchy
15 Actuary
16 Aridity
19 Usual
20 Koran
21 Speed

94

Across
1 Litter
4 Rally
8 Staff
9 Pelican
10 Espouse
11 Hype
12 Leg
14 Lean
15 Ulna
18 Tip
21 Fuji
23 Allergy
25 Compost
26 Bjorn
27 Thyme
28 Meekly

Down
1 Listen
2 Traipse
3 Effluent
4 Rile
5 Lucky
6 Yankee
7 Spiel
13 Gullible
16 Norfolk
17 Offcut
19 Pasta
20 Sydney
22 Jemmy
24 Lone

95

Across
1 Adore
4 Handel
9 Integer
10 Bingo
11 Urns
12 Viscera
13 Ale
14 Open
16 Erse
18 Odd
20 Strewed
21 Able
24 Inner
25 Unwound
26 Onside
27 Tutor

Down
1 Adieus
2 Often
3 Edge
5 Ambushed
6 Dangers
7 Loofah
8 Grave
13 Answered
15 Parents
17 Eskimo
18 Odour
19 Bender
22 Blunt
23 Swat

96

Across
1 Roger
4 Sand
8 Hammers
9 Stein
10 Basie
11 Inspect
13 Starry
15 Portal
17 Lusting
20 Views
22 On ice
23 Allegro
24 Stet
25 Extol

Down
1 Rehab
2 Gamesmanship
3 Roe-deer
4 Sushi
5 Noses
6 Seventy-eight
7 Instil
12 Nip
13 Salmon
14 Yen
16 Orville
18 Inept
19 Giant
21 Spoil

97

Across
1 Holland
5 Daze
7 Sauce
8 Steamy
10 Echo
11 Cressida
13 Indeed
14 Unesco
17 Aesthete
19 Ogen
21 Alumni
22 Aioli
23 Gall
24 Tartare

Down
1 Hysterical
2 Laughed
3 Apex
4 Desire
5 Dressing
6 Zombi
9 Mayonnaise
12 Bechamel
15 Signora
16 Strict
18 Salsa
20 Parr

98

Across
1 Backer
4 Hoarse
7 Centipede
9 Iron
10 Slip
11 Steep
13 Settee
14 Rescue
15 Agrees
17 Scythe
19 Reach
20 Bred
22 Gone
23 Direction
24 Rattle
25 Hearty

Down
1 Babies
2 Keen
3 Rotate
4 Hopper
5 Adds
6 Elapse
7 Contorted
8 Elocution
11 Sever
12 Peach
15 Ambler
16 Severe
17 Scotch
18 Energy
21 Diet
22 Goya

99

Across
7 Assert
8 Auntie
10 Bearing
11 Nacre
12 Glee
13 Bound
17 Break
18 Halo
22 Acrid
23 Contain
24 Picked
25 Gather

Down
1 Garbage
2 Ashamed
3 Trail
4 Cunning
5 Stock
6 Rebel
9 Ignorance
14 Grudges
15 Panache
16 Foundry
19 Happy
20 Trick
21 Sneak

100

Across

1 Walking
5 Shoos
8 Chaff
9 Fondant
10 Animate
11 Twerp
12 Tights
14 Brazen
17 Amber
19 Crampon
22 Fanfare
23 Among
24 Close
25 Address

Down

1 Wicca
2 Leaning
3 Infra
4 Gaffer
5 Senator
6 Ovate
7 Set upon
12 Traffic
13 Terrace
15 Zip code
16 Eczema
18 Bingo
20 Award
21 Negus

101

Across

1 Grabs
4 Holed
10 Cabbage
11 Impel
12 Putti
13 Eagerly
15 Nile
17 Brags
19 Overt
22 Lane
25 Bootleg
27 Rolls
29 Daily
30 Thistle
31 Agile
32 Pylon

Down

2 Rabat
3 Bearing
5 Owing
6 Emperor
7 Scope
8 Jewel
9 Slays
14 Aeon
16 Isle
18 Rioting
20 Versify
21 Abode
23 Agate
24 Ashen
26 Loyal
28 Lotto

102

Across

1 Chef
5 Hawn
7 Imitate
8 Boutique
10 Vase
12 Otis
14 Istanbul
16 Sinister
17 Yoga
18 Jest
19 Spinster
22 Exclude
23 Pass
24 Zany

Down

1 Crab
2 Fiat
3 Disquiet
4 Safe
5 Heavenly
6 Nape
9 Outline
11 Smuggle
13 Skittles
15 Terminus
18 Jump
19 Sack
20 Suez
21 Ruby

103

Across

1 Piers
5 Of the
8 Realm
9 Elemi
10 Leningrad
11 Lip
12 Tinderboxes
15 Self-assured
19 Elm
20 Doubleton
22 Expel
23 Rufus
24 Erred
25 Spitz

Down

1 Peerless
2 Exempt
3 Sri Lanka
4 Sarnie
5 Omen
6 Thorax
7 Eked
13 Baroness
14 Schmaltz
16 Louder
17 Set off
18 Delphi
20 Duke
21 Lord

104

Across

4 Sister
5 Shun
7 Vaulted
10 Jolts
11 Mariner
12 Zebra
14 Requiem
15 Yemen
16 Ripened
20 Vixen
21 Delight
22 Hoot
23 Avocet

Down

1 Psalm
2 Fever
3 Theorem
4 Swag
6 Nature
8 Taken in
9 Diluted
10 Jezebel
13 Zenith
14 Reredos
17 Nerve
18 Disco
19 Chat